Ready • Set • Date

By

Jonathan & David Bennett, Lori Ann Davis, MA, Melette Evans, Jennifer Gaynor-Yaker, Geoff Laughton, Jerry McQuay, Laura Menze, Joanna Shakti, Dena Skoko, Sheryl Spangler, Terrance Tomsha.

© 2019 BC Movie, LLC – Rampant Feline Media

All rights reserved. No portion of this book may be reproduced in any form without permission from the publisher, except as permitted by U.S. copyright law.

For permissions contact:

betsy@betsychasse.net

www.rampantfelinemedia.com

Contents

Betsy Chasse 1

Introduction: By Betsy Chasse 2

Lori Ann Davis: 4

Certified Relationship Coach-Author-Speaker 4

Dating after divorce for women: By Lori Ann Davis 6

Jerry McQuay 15

Dating After Divorce: By Jerry McQuay 16

David and Jonathan Bennett 25

Dating with Kids: By David and Jonathan Bennett 27

Lori Ann Davis 35

Certified Relationship Coach-Author-Speaker 35

Dating with Kids for Moms: By Lori Ann Davis 37

Dena Skoko 45

Dating after a Toxic Relationship By Dena Skoko 46

Geoff Laughton 53

Dating After A Toxic Relationship –How Do I Search for Peace After Going Through Hell?: By Geoff Laughton 54

Laura Menze 63

Ready for Marriage 64

Never Been Married and You're Finally Ready for the One! – For Women: By Laura Menze 64

Jennifer Gaynor-Yaker 75

Mastering the Art of Online Dating (so you can find "The One"): By Jennifer Gaynor-Yaker 76

Melette Evans: "Helping create happier lives one person at a time" 83

Marry Who You Want, Not Who You Need: By Melette Evans 85

Terance Tomsha 94

Never married, ready for marriage: By Terrance Tomsha 95

Sheryl Spangler 105

HOW TO BE A SUCCESSFUL ONLINE DATER: By Sheryl Spangler 106

Joanna Shakti The Soul Love Mentor of Ecstatic Intimacy . 116

Intimacy: The Glue that Binds: By Joanna Shakti 118

BETSY CHASSE

Betsy Chasse is an award-winning filmmaker (What The Bleep Do We Know?!, Song of The New Earth, Pregnant In America), best-selling author (Tipping Sacred Cows, Dancing In The Unknown, It Came out of my Vagina, Now What?!) and mom. After her divorce she decided to figure out how to date successfully and created the web series Radical Dating, based on the work of David Steele a relationship coaching expert. Due to the success of Radical Dating she is now is development of a new series Ready • Set • Date, which explores further, how to successfully date in order to find your true love. Betsy is currently still seeking and happily single, but is optimistic!

www.betsychase.net

Introduction
By Betsy Chasse

In 2011, after 10 years of marriage, I became a statistic. A single mom, 41 years old and not quite ready to be single. After a year of getting my life together I decided I'd go for it. I set up my online dating profile and dreamed that Mr. Right would show up in my inbox.

Sigh… that is not what happened.

What happened was weeks and weeks of waves, winks, messages from men who had clearly not read my profile, men who probably were not who they said they were, endless messaging without dates, or dates set up and cancelled. That doesn't even cover the terrible dates I actually went on!

What was I doing wrong? Why was this dating thing so hard? Curiosity is what drives my projects and I decided to find out what I was doing wrong and fix it. After searching through relationship and dating sites, reading books and talking with hundreds of coaches, I realized that the truth was, I didn't know how to date! I spend more time researching my doctors than I do the men I might want to go out with, I had no idea what I really wanted in a relationship, I had ideas, but hadn't really done the work to become clear on my requirements, needs and wants (something you'll learn about in this book).

I learned that dating can either suck or it can be a fun, productive way to find a lasting partner.

That's why I created this book, to help you learn the tools needed to find success in love. It may sound horribly unsexy and unromantic to consider approaching dating like you would a business proposition but think about it. Your relationship has a huge impact on every aspect of your life, don't you want it to be right? You deserve it to be everything you desire and more and in order to achieve that, you need to be willing to put in the work, be committed to the outcome you require and be willing to hold out until you get it.

This book covers many of the situations we all find ourselves in, dating after divorce, dating as a single parent, dating after a toxic relationship, how to create an online profile that reflects who you really are and what you really want, and the tools needed to date, and eventually find the relationship that is right for you.

One of the greatest lessons I have learned exploring dating is that I needed to do a lot of work on myself before I could actually find the right person for me. The more I understood myself, emptied out of bunch of old suitcases of stuff that wasn't serving me, and got clarity on what I truly wanted, the more successful I was at choosing dates.

Dating doesn't have to suck, it can be fun, follow the tips and tools in this book and you'll find your path.

Lori Ann Davis: Certified Relationship Coach-Author-Speaker

I have a unique and passionate approach to love and relationships and believe that everyone deserves and can have the relationship of their dreams.

Bringing you the benefits of 30 years of experience. I work with women who are struggling to find happiness in their relationships. They would like to attract and keep their ideal partner but have not yet been successful.

I help women tap into the power of feminine energy and use the Law of Attraction to enhance not only their relationships but their lives.

I will guide you every step of the way: getting ready for love, attracting a date, creating successful first dates, moving toward intimacy, deciding if he is the one, and growing the relationship.

I will provide you with insights and secrets from my personal experiences, proven tools, tips and techniques that create fast results. I will motivate you, inspire you, teach you, and coach you on your journey.

I am the author of Unmasking Secrets to Unstoppable Relationships: How to Find, Keep and Renew Love and Passion in Your Life.

I am also one of the coaches on the new Radical Dating Show.

www.LoriAnnDavis.com

DATING AFTER DIVORCE FOR WOMEN
By Lori Ann Davis

Divorce can be a traumatic event to go through. Dating after divorce can feel daunting and stressful. "When should I start dating?", "What type of man do I want to date?" "Where do I meet them?" These are some of the questions singles ask me every day.

"When should I start dating after divorce?" The answer is unique to each person. Some of you might be ready to date while you are going through the divorce process while others may not be ready still years after the divorce is final. The important choice is to date when YOU feel ready.

Dating when you are still angry or bitter from your divorce can lead to attracting other angry, bitter men. Dating when you are feeling hurt or victimized by your ex, can open you up to meeting others who are similar to your ex. This is the Law of Attraction at work. What is the Law of Attraction? Simply put, it is a universal law that says we will attract into our lives what we focus on. Whether it is positive or negative, whether you are aware of it or not, every thought you have and every emotion you feel affects your reality. That can seem overwhelming, but with a little conscious work, you can get out in front of your thoughts and emotions and start attracting the man you want.

How do you know you are ready? Unpacking your own personal baggage is the first step. Everyone, who has been in a relationship, has some baggage. People who say they don't are in denial! The key is to do some soul searching and to get some help if you need it to work through as much of the anger, hurt, or resentment from your marriage. It is important to heal what went wrong in the past relationship before entering into a new one.

A perfect place to start is to become aware of your thoughts. I suggest you spend some time making a list of all the thoughts and beliefs you have about dating, men, and marriage. Write it all down, don't censor yourself or feel bad about what might seem like some really negative thoughts. If you don't write them down and become aware of them, how can you shift them? Making this list will give you an idea of which ones need your attention. Remember, you get what you focus on. How often are you thinking thoughts that are not taking you in the direction you want to go? Probably more often than you realize.

Here are some thoughts or beliefs you might have:

- ❖ What happened in the past is what will happen in the future.
- ❖ Relationships take too much work.

- ❖ I don't believe a loving, healthy relationship is possible.
- ❖ No one is going to be faithful.
- ❖ I have to give up what is important to me to be in a relationship.
- ❖ Men only want sex.
- ❖ There are no good men out there.
- ❖ I will get hurt if I open my heart to a man.

Now it's your turn. I suspect you found at least one in that list that fits, however what other thoughts and beliefs do you have about men and relationships?

Letting go of past experiences and forgiving others and ourselves, is an important part of moving forward. What did you learn from your marriage? What did you learn about yourself? What was the silver lining in this experience? Yes, there is always one; you just might have to dig deep to find it. It is important at this stage to stop blaming others, even if you are justified in feeling hurt, angry, or betrayed, carrying that with you will drag you down. It makes it hard, if not impossible, to move forward. Freedom comes from forgiving our past and ourselves. As you consciously make a choice to choose better thoughts and let go of your past, you will feel like a huge weight lifted.

Now you can start replacing those negative thoughts and beliefs with more empowering ones. Empowering thoughts are the ones that make you feel good, motivate you, and make you feel more confident.

Some ideas to get you started:

- ❖ I deserve love in my life.
- ❖ The man I seek is also seeking me.
- ❖ I am relaxed and have fun on dates.
- ❖ I am closer to finding my soulmate every day.
- ❖ I open my heart and trust that love will follow.
- ❖ With new tools and skills, I create a different relationship experience.
- ❖ There are loving, caring, faithful partners and I am one.

These positive thoughts and affirmations help you focus on what a good relationship looks and feels like. Keeping your focus on the positive is an important step keeping you from falling back into old habits and repeating the past.

When you are focusing on empowering thoughts, don't limit them to dating and relationships. Be sure to look at how you feel about yourself. How can you attract an amazing partner if you don't feel amazing about yourself? It is time to make a list of all the things that make you a great person. What do you have to offer? When you are aware of your strengths, you will date with more confidence and will allow your authentic self to show through. It is time to love yourself!

Here are some ideas to get you started:

- ❖ I am worthy of love.
- ❖ I am confident in what I have to offer a partner.
- ❖ I effortlessly radiate positive energy.
- ❖ I am comfortable with who I am.
- ❖ The more I love myself, the more I attract my ideal partner.
- ❖ I am loveable and worthy of receiving love.

Once you are ready to stick your toe back into the dating pool, how do you get started? How do you date in today's complicated dating world? So much may have changed since you last dated.

Most singles go out looking for a partner with a vague idea of what they want in a relationship. This is like heading out on a trip without a map and hoping you get there. Chances are you will end up someplace you didn't want to go or just drive around, lost indefinitely. That is why many singles become frustrated with dating. You need a road map for dating just as you do for a trip.

It is important to identify what you truly want. Become clear about the kind of relationship and the qualities in a partner you are looking for. I do not mean superficial things like height, hair color, hobbies, and the shopping list some singles have. I mean the core values and life vision you must have in common for the relationship to work.

After a divorce, you may not know what you want in a relationship, but you might have some idea what you don't want! This is a good place to start. Look at any past relationships you have had and make a list of the things you liked and didn't like about the relationship. Remember, we always want to focus on the positives, so we attract those into our lives. Take the things you don't want to repeat in the next relationship and turn them into what you do want.

For example, in your marriage you and your husband had difficulties resolving problems and communicating. You might be tempted to say, "I don't want a partner who can't express his needs or disappears to his man cave every time I want to talk!" What you do want is a partner you can talk to easily and a relationship where you can settle differences peacefully.

Once you start dating, you will learn even more about what you like and don't like in a partner. This is where you must be willing to get out there, be brave, and get out of you comfort zone. Start meeting people with the idea of learning more about them and yourself. It is ok to create your vision and your desires as you go along. Start with what you know and add to it as you date and learn more about yourself and what you truly desire. I encourage you to be open to your ideal partner coming in a package that is different than you expected.

Not that long ago, I was single after being married for 28 years. The idea of dating was scary, but I was determined to have love in my life again. Every night before going to bed. I would spend time living in that relationship I was creating. I could not only imagine it, but I could feel it, as if it was already there. I truly believed my partner was on his way to me and it was just a matter of time before we were together.

I was not sure when or how, but I knew I would be successful, and I was.

I am now happily remarried because of that belief!

To attract your ideal partner and have the relationship you desire, you must first believe you can have it!

The next step is to be able to hold on to that belief, even before it shows up in your life. One way to help you stay focused on the outcome you are looking for is to write it down. Be as specific as you can and remember to tap into the feeling of what it will be like when your ideal partner is part of your life. What will you do together? How will you feel? Create an image in your mind that you can see and feel. Now hold that image and spend time with it daily as you plan inspired actions that will put you in a position to meet new people. Keep moving forward holding this vision until you are successful. If you do this, you will find your partner.

It takes courage to date again, to be ready to open your heart and be vulnerable again. At some point, you just have to get out there and start dating. Date with an attitude of curiosity. This is a learning experience for you. Realize you will run into men who are not right for you. We all do! It is part of putting yourself out there and meeting new people. The experience of dating is a great learning tool. It will show you quickly what you still need to work on in your own thoughts and beliefs. It will show you what you like and don't like. If you notice a pattern in who you are meeting, this is a guide to show you what baggage you are still carrying around that needs to be released. There are no bad experiences just opportunities to learn and grow.

Divorce can and often is a blessing in disguise. This is a wonderful opportunity for you to not just fall in love but to actively participate in creating love and a relationship that you desire. Don't rush the process. Take things slow and really get to know a person before making any decisions. Learn to accept people for who they are without trying to change them. Be prepared to be patient and not set a time limit on finding your next partner. Make sure that as you are dating, you are also living a life that you love. You probably have more free time now that you are divorced. It is the perfect time to try a new hobby, make new friends, take more time to do what you want, and create a life you love. Then when you do find that perfect partner for you, he will be a wonderful addition to your already happy life.

Most importantly be gentle with yourself, some days will be better than others and most dates will not lead you to your next Mr. Right. Time is on your side, create your life, your way, develop deeper friendships and connections to fill your heart with the love you desire and when you do meet him, he'll fit right in.

Jerry McQuay

Jerry is an artist and a post-divorce expert. He has co-facilitated a divorce support group for 15 years. Part of the important work he does with the group focuses on dating after divorce. Jerry believes that casual dating after divorce is fine but it's important to do self-growth work prior to embarking on a significant post-divorce relationship.

When Jerry's 20-year marriage ended, he sought out resources to help him move through the devastating experience of divorce. Through personal therapy work and a divorce support group, he was able to move forward to rebuild his life and self-esteem.

Today he is happily remarried to his soul mate, and they live in Charlotte, NC.

Jerry can be reached at jerryhpuck@gmail.com.

Dating After Divorce
By Jerry McQuay

After my 20-year marriage, including a wonderful teenage daughter, ended in 2003, I was in shock and awe that my world was crumbling, and my "life" was over. Guess what? That "life" WAS over. It took a great deal of work to first accept that fact, then "grow" myself enough to get to a good place emotionally.

Perhaps, the first thing I learned after divorce and doing the autopsy of my past marriage is that our ex has nothing to do with our own healing. Then, we begin to realize our part in the ending of that relationship and learn to "own our crap". Do we have baggage? You're darn right, we do because we have been living our life. My favorite Match.com headline is "I HAVE NO BAGGAGE". Yeah- right.

I attribute my success of reaching "successful singleness" to my support system including a divorce support group, a wonderful therapist, positive support from family and friends and to my outlet- my art and my painting. Doing any or all of these things will help you heal.

Dating after divorce is a journey in and of itself. It's different than dating when you were much younger and looking for your first partner. You've lived a whole lot more and your needs are different.

Although there were many dating partners during my single days... most were fleeting, as is to be expected, and each one taught me something about myself, and what kind of partner I truly wanted.

Before mentioning the more meaningful relationships, I had a bizarre experience early in my "new dating career"- I met a lady I'll call, Joan. I found an ad from the back of a local Rag Mag dating line... many phone conversations for a week or so... she was flirtatious to say the least... many titillating suggestions coming from her that were very stimulating. Finally- we were able to meet at restaurant across town. I was so anxious as I drove across the city to finally meet Joan. I was anxious because we only met on the phone and we had never seen each other. As I approached her, she suddenly waved her hand pointing at my head-to-toe and shouts "Oh no!" She mumbles her disgust of me standing there as she quickly gets back in her car and screeches tires out of the parking lot to get away from me! I was shocked as I'm a reasonably nice-looking guy. I kept thinking, "what was that???" I had a hellish ride back across town because my ego had just taken a major blow! It took a few days, then I realized she was on some weird trip and I didn't want any of that anyway... Besides, she really was not all that! I soon learned that dating is not that insane... surely this dating thing will get better than that. It took a while but from this bizarre experience, I did learn that I'm OK... that I will be OK... and my dating life will be OK.

Shortly thereafter, I dated a lady- I'll call her Ann. I met her organically through a friend. She was younger and quite needy emotionally. She would call with some personal concern and sometimes crisis and I recall feeling so good because I felt wanted and needed. The relationship was also very sexual, which "stroked" my ego and made the drama "worthwhile". This relationship endured for a couple of years off and on. I remember one amusing story about Ann. As we say in the south, bless her heart, she wasn't the brightest and to be fair, she was young and naive. I got tickets to a Panthers NFL football game... we settled in our seats and as the game began, she asked me where is the yellow line? You know- the on-screen TV graphics... I laughed out loud until I realized she was serious.

We had many good times, but as time went by and I continued to "grow-up", emotionally, her neediness became less and less attractive. It was then that I realized that this relationship was not functional, so I ended it. She had become invested and she got very upset with me, but it needed to end.

As I reflected on this relationship, I realized the reason her neediness felt so good to me early on was because I, myself was very needy!

Also, I learned about how Ann's type of "love" is "other-centered"... when we cause our partner to be the reason for our own happiness. I also realized that I had been "guilty" of the same in my previous marriage. For those of us that allow our romantic relationships to be "other-centered", we will be more negatively impacted when that relationship ends. From this relationship, I learned the value of investing into self-growth which leads to a greater self-love and not needing to feel "validated" by my partner. I also learned that I wanted the same in return from a future partner.

A year or so passed as I continued to blaze my trail, and then I met a lovely lady- I'll call her Betty.

We met on a radio station romance line (weird- right?) and we were attracted to each other. We went out a couple of times, when I soon learned we would become physical fairly quickly. I remember how flattered I was, and I enjoyed the release! Betty was advancing this relationship rather quickly and I went along for the ride! I had met her 17-year-old son- he and I got along fine.

After several months of dating, Betty and I were at dinner and she said her son suggested that his Mom "come clean" with me concerning her past. I was eagerly listening to her truth when she revealed, that at 39 years-old, she had been married 5 times! I realized why we were "advancing" so quickly, and I also knew I did not want to be #6! That was the last time I saw her. I called her the next day and explained my side and it ended well. I remember feeling at that time that, for her, I suppose the "what" (new marriage) was more important than the "who".

From this relationship with Betty, I realized I am a people-pleaser. In this and previous relationships (including my 20-year marriage), I was very willing to "go along" and didn't typically exercise boundaries. More importantly, I didn't even know what my boundaries were! I did realize from Betty a red flag boundary deal-breaker when I learned the news of her past and I felt strong when I ended that relationship.

Some time passed as I continued doing my thing, including painting and showing my art. I invested in a working studio and displayed my art in a gallery for the first time in my life! I kept that studio for 10 years and learned so much about people from that experience. I began giving back to the divorce support group and grew to eventually facilitating the meetings! I also gained new friendships and raised my daughter and began feeling a contentment in my singleness.

After a long break, I decided to return to online dating. I meet a lady, Cathy on E Harmony. We dated for a year and a half. There was much to enjoy and learn from that relationship. I remember sharing with Cathy about how our conversations were so meaningful. We related very well on "meaning of life" stuff. I joked about the contrast how my much younger self would relate with my new wife in the early 80's. Our biggest connection was being young and "in lust" and the advent of MTV!

Dating Cathy was quite a growth relationship for me. She appreciated growing our "EQ" (Emotional Quotient). I feel like we learned much from each other. We often discussed the importance of "being in the moment" during this time and not "future-basing" this romance. Cathy was intrigued with our conversations as she was dealing with some remnants from her long previous marriage. We were able to converse about removing masks and becoming our true selves. I gained on that endeavor in many ways and quite frankly, many times for the first time in my life!

As time moved on, we both realized we were not a good fit long-term- especially our different personalities. As I like to speak to the divorce group, a favorite saying of mine is "Opposites attract.... divorce".

I learned from ending the romance with Cathy that we both were able to practice "healthy termination". In fact, we're Facebook friends today!

I also learned from my time with Cathy that I no longer wanted to partner with a critical personality type. That became a deal-breaker for me, and I realized a new requirement for me is a less demanding and more accepting "sweetheart" personality. I also learned to embrace my quirky self and my best partner would accept me, quirks and all.

After dating Cathy for a year and a half, I broke it off and decided that this was a good time to rest from dating for a while. By this time, I felt very comfortable in my singleness and I didn't NEED a partner. It felt good to be present for my daughter as she endured college, work my job, paint and show my art, enjoy my family and friends and that was enough. This single life thing is a really good thing!

A year or so later, I did jump back into dating. I felt I was more self-aware and had learned requirements (must haves) in a new relationship after my experiences. I also felt fresh, relaxed and that I could embrace the adventure of online dating!

Here's a helpful hint, "clean up" your social media, particularly if you overly state some political views... they may not accurately reflect on you.

In early 2012, I finally focused on what I wanted in a partner. First- a lovely person inside and out, a sweetheart and one that is self-aware. I had a memorable conversation with a good friend on a Sunday in January about how I'd like to have someone special on my arm for my daughter's wedding coming up in June. That conversation helped me gain clarity to my desires in my partner. I will always fondly remember sharing with and learning from my friend Bill that day.

I carried forward my newfound focus and things began to come into alignment. Just a couple of months later, I met the loveliest, sweetest, smartest woman I know, Sheryl. We did it right, in that after emailing through the site and "connecting", we had a phone call to hear voices and learn about our conversational styles, which is very helpful for both parties. Soon after we met. It went very well, and I quickly remembered a friend's advice, if you are into her, to "always have a plan", i.e. next date. I made sure to do just that and Sheryl and I saw each other often. We became great friends and then, romantically connected.

Just a few months later, she agreed with a leap of faith to accompany me to my daughter's out of town wedding. Not only did we have a blast, but, she, my future wife, the woman I so dearly love with all my heart caught the bouquet at my daughter's wedding!

I learned much in the divorce recovery support group. I became a big fan of the book, "Rebuilding- When Your Relationship Ends", by Dr. Bill Fisher and Dr. Robert Alberti. I gained so much from this body of work and highly recommend this book to anyone who is ending a relationship- particularly those that are longer term.

Also, Meetup groups offer many types of meetings, discussions and social events for singles, and they can be extremely beneficial.

In the "Rebuilding" work, there is a chapter called "Relatedness" about how having dating partners that create "growing relationships" will help both partners gain better self-awareness. Some of the keys in these romantic relationships are to not "future" base and to stay in the present. We begin to realize the emphasis is more on "real life" stuff, than fluff and fantasy that past relationships may have included.

Also, there are pitfalls to pay attention to, including, not making your partner responsible for your own happiness, not over-investing and neglecting other relationships, and incorrectly thinking you will never have another great romance if this one doesn't work out.

There are numerous benefits to casually dating after divorce, including contrasting and comparing, which helps you find out what you prefer. This new knowledge will help lead to learning your own boundaries, requirements, needs and wants. Also, a functional relationship can be a "laboratory for growth". We gain an opportunity for true maturity that feels very good.

Perhaps my favorite passage from the "Rebuilding" book around a benefit from "growing relationships" is, "You will be able to have healthy relationships if you choose, because you are learning to have a better relationship with yourself".

David and Jonathan Bennett

David and Jonathan Bennett are dating and relationship experts with over 15 years of combined experience helping men and women find love.

After years informally helping friends and family with dating, in 2012, they founded "The Popular Man" to help paid clients find relationship success. The next year, they partnered with local matchmakers to expand their services.

In 2017, they founded "Double Trust Dating," (https://doubletrustdating.com/) a full service dating and relationship business where they use their extensive experience and education to provide coaching, events, courses, and general support services to create meaningful, quality relationships.

They are authors of seven books on dating, relationships, and personal success. They are both certified counselors in Ohio, with backgrounds in psychology, business, and education. They both earned degrees from Ohio University and Emory University, graduating at top of their classes. They are members of Phi Beta Kappa, the prestigious honor society.

They have appeared on various radio and television shows and have been used as trusted sources in over 600 media appearances, including Men's Health, The Wall Street Journal,

Redbook, Brides, Men's Journal, and Prevention. They regularly speak to business, civic, and student groups on topics related to relationships and personal success.

Dating with Kids
By David and Jonathan Bennett

With the increase in divorce, the high number of births outside of marriage, and fathers receiving more custodial rights, the number of singles dads has increased exponentially in recent years. In fact, the number of households headed by single dads has risen 900% since the 1960s*.

So, if you feel like you're weird or abnormal navigating the dating world as a single father, realize that there are many other men doing the exact same thing. And, because it's very common, the people you're meeting and wanting to date won't be as shocked as you might assume. We promise!

Even though it's more widespread, navigating the dating scene as a single dad still presents many challenges. While it might not be dating on "hard mode," it's not exactly easy either.

It's difficult to be a parent, even a part-time one, and find time to commit to dating someone or even finding a partner. Parenthood takes a lot of your resources, including money, time, and emotional energy. Of course, this assumes you have a reliable sitter to even give you a dating life!

And, we'll be blunt. Having children can scare off potential partners who'd otherwise be head over heels for you.

However, despite the obvious drawbacks, being a single dad isn't a dating death sentence.

Online dating app Zoosk's own data suggest that 83% of their female users would date a single dad **. And, being a supportive single dad who is active in the lives of your children makes you more likely to get into a relationship. Yes, the research shows that women find taking care of your child pretty attractive. In fact, one study showed that women are more three times as likely to give you their phone number if they see you actively caring for a young child.

The following are practical tips and insights that we've developed and learned, not only as dating coaches, but also as single dads who have successfully gotten into meaningful relationships. So, if you're trying to find love as a single dad, this chapter will make your life a lot easier.

First, we want to address the role of your child in the dating game. You are, in a way, "dating for two." And, that can be confusing and intimidating for many men.

As we mentioned, the research shows that for men at least, being a single parent is considered generally positive. But many guys notice the child talk can make a woman's heart melt. And, they take it too far. Intentionally or not, they start to use their kids as "props," which is manipulative and unfair to both your child and your potential partner.

Our female clients have been reporting that single dads on dating apps are really hamming it up about what great dads they are, and it's getting a little obvious they are doing it because they think women want to hear that.

Nothing is more unattractive than viewing your own child as a means to get a date. In addition, telling everyone what a great dad you are means nothing. We definitely want you to be a great dad to your child. And, you can certainly let your date see that. But, show her over time. Don't tell her in a dating profile or in a long-winded first date conversation.

The opposite of using your kid as a "prop" is hiding that you're a father, whether deliberately trying to mislead potential partners, or not being proud of your child. That isn't authentic either. And, few people are going to accept you hiding the fact you're a father until a much later date.

Finally, we want to address something that is very widespread. Even though you're "dating for two" in a way, you want the process of dating and getting into a relationship to be focused on you. We've had clients in the past who only talked about their children to the point you'd think their only interests involved parenting.

Your date ultimately isn't going to fall for your child. She's going to have to discover your unique interests, goals, and find you attractive. And, if all you talk about is little Johnny's baseball games or Susie's first words, she might fall for your kid, but not you. Or, she might just go out with someone else.

You definitely want her to love your child! But, if it's going to be a real romantic relationship, she'll have to fall for you first. Don't attempt to do it the other way around.

So, when you make your dating profile or meet potential dates, you can mention your child. But, stick more to conversations and information about yourself and your interests, at least in the beginning. Then, as time goes on and you get closer to her, you can share more about your child.

We've talked a lot about your kid and how he or she plays into the dating game. Now it's time to talk about your role since, as we mentioned, it's the most important. Even if your son or daughter is super cute and amazing, that won't get you very far.

Since balancing work, parenting, and all of life's other issues can be tough, a lot of guys have, simply put, "let themselves go," at least to a degree. And, while that's to be expected, if you want to date a quality woman, you're going to need to be quality yourself. The basic rule for dating as a single dad is really the same as all dating: be as broadly attractive as possible.

Assessing your attractiveness can be challenging and requires a lot of brutal honesty. You might look in the mirror and have a hard time accepting that the fun-loving, charismatic, fitter version of yourself is just a memory. But, if you want to be your most successful in dating, you'll want to find ways you can be your most attractive.

Many guys get angry when they hear this, thinking we're trying to change them. And, we are! But, it's actually a good thing. The traits considered attractive in dating are also ones that will help you succeed in all other areas of life.

So, don't think of self-improvement as changing your core values because it's not. Think of it as tapping your full potential to be a great man and father. And, it has the side effect of making you all that much more irresistible.

This chapter is too short to go into great detail about the basics of attraction. However, it can be summed up as this: be excellent! Get healthy. Dress for success. Be funny, witty, and charming. Walk and act with confidence. Be honest, vulnerable, and assertive. Take risks. See the humor in everything.

Go out and reach for the stars in your work, hobbies, and general pursuits. Put down your phone and mindfully enjoy all moments, especially those with loved ones in your life. You'd be amazed how even these small changes will attract the right romantic relationships and bigger opportunities for success.

Finally, we want to address a few issues related to the practical aspects of dating as a single father.

First, get a reliable sitter! Making a relationship work requires time and energy. And, you need to do a lot of that without your kids around. Having to scramble for a sitter or bugging reluctant relatives just makes dating even more stressful.

We've found that people without a reliable sitter often give up on dating since the stress and aggravation of finding someone to watch their kids is too much hassle. And, if you have to constantly cancel or reschedule with your dates, they will just give up on even seeing you.

Second, take some time for yourself. This means finding time to hit the gym, read a good book, and, yes, go on dates. Many single parents of both sexes feel guilty putting themselves before their children, even temporarily. And, even the best of kids will use that guilt to get their way.

However, don't fall for that temptation. As long as your child is well taken care of, properly supervised, and you're active in his or her life, then you shouldn't feel guilty about setting aside time for yourself. And, that includes dating. If your son or daughter makes an issue of it, politely, but firmly set boundaries.

Third, when trying to get into a great relationship, we advise keeping an open mind and not overthinking anything, especially in the beginning. When you go on a date, try to be mindful and get to know the person in front of you, rather than letting your worries about the future overtake you.

Obviously if your date is clearly bad for your child, you should not pursue anything else. But, if you just met a cool, fun, attractive person, don't sabotage it or overthink it. Give it a chance!

Also, this is a great place to add that you don't have to just limit yourself to dating other single parents. You might find a single mom who hates the idea of another child in her life. Likewise, it's possible there is a childless person who would feel enriched by the idea of dating a single dad. Consider people as individuals and don't be too quick to assume one way or another how someone will feel about you and your children.

However, having said that, it's best not to bring too many people you date into your child's life unless you feel some level of commitment. Too many children are scarred by their mom or dad bringing an endless parade of new partners around. The kids would develop a bond, only to have that person ripped away.

So, while you need to go with the flow and not write someone off, wait until you've decided that you're both ready for some exclusivity before inviting your partner to develop a deeper relationship with your kids.

A lot of people ask us about exact numbers. For many people, an ideal wait would be about a month. But the key is that you're committed enough to not introduce this new person, encourage a bond with your kids, then jerk that person away, only to start the cycle all over again. And, sadly, many single parents put their kids through this.

We want to wish you the best in dating as a single dad. It's great to see guys step up as fathers and contribute to a better future for the world. And, since you can never have too much love in your life, go out and find an amazing, high quality relationship that will make you and your entire family happier.

(http://www.pewsocialtrends.org/2013/07/02/the-rise-of-single-fathers/)

(https://www.zoosk.com/date-mix/dating-statistics-and-research/dating-statistics/single-dads/)

Lori Ann Davis
Certified Relationship Coach-Author-Speaker

I have a unique and passionate approach to love and relationships and believe that everyone deserves and can have the relationship of their dreams.

Bringing you the benefits of 30 years of experience. I work with women who are struggling to find happiness in their relationships. They would like to attract and keep their ideal partner but have not yet been successful.

I help women tap into the power of feminine energy and use the Law of Attraction to enhance not only their relationships but their lives.

I will guide you every step of the way: getting ready for love, attracting a date, creating successful first dates, moving toward intimacy, deciding if he is the one, and growing the relationship.

I will provide you with insights and secrets from my personal experiences, proven tools, tips and techniques that create fast results. I will motivate you, inspire you, teach you, and coach you on your journey.

I am the author of Unmasking Secrets to Unstoppable Relationships: How to Find, Keep and Renew Love and Passion in Your Life.

I am also one of the coaches on the new Radical Dating Show.

www.LoriAnnDavis.com

Dating with Kids for Moms
By Lori Ann Davis

I was a single mom not that long ago, so I understand firsthand the challenges children add to the dating process. It is complicated enough to sort out your own requirements in finding a partner, but when you add the welfare of your children to the mix, there is so much more to consider. Your time is also limited when you have children to take care of, so you need to make the most of the time you do have. You also have to talk to your children about dating.

That is a lot added to the already daunting idea of dating again after a divorce.

At some point, you will feel the desire to date again and having children to consider does not have to stand in your way. I am going to give you some guidelines that will help you navigate your way through the dating world as a single mom.

Are you ready to date?

This should be the first consideration. Dating when you are not over your ex and have not dealt with the emotions related to your divorce can lead to dating experiences that are not ideal. Two people who are hurt or still have unfinished business from the past, do not make a good couple. You bring your unfinished business into the new relationship. Know you why for dating and be clear about your wants, needs, values and beliefs. Never date out of desperation or loneliness. There are other ways to get those needs met. Adding more friends to your life might be a better option. For more information on this topic, read my chapter, Dating after Divorce for Women.

Do you have a stable life for you and your children?

This does not mean you have to have everything perfect. I do suggest you take some time after your divorce to get into a routine with your new life as a single parent. When you feel comfortable in this role then you are ready to add a new dimension to your life.

Are your children ready for you to date?

Sit down with and talk to them before you start to date. They will have their own reactions to your dating. Learn to distinguish between their needs and their wants regarding you being in another relationship. For instance, they might not want you to date at all because they are still hoping you will get back together with their father. It is very common for children to want their parents back together. They might need more quality time with you. Your children might feel insecure about their relationship with you and their relationship with their father. Before you start dating again, sit down with them and talk about how they feel, what they need, what they want, what they fear, and what they hope. Prepare yourself for whatever comes up so you can listen without judgement. More than likely they will have ambivalent feelings. If at first, they express feelings of anger and express a desire for you not to date, allow them to share those feelings. Then spend some time talking to them trying to find out what is underneath those feelings. If it is a fear, you can reassure them that you will still spend plenty of time with them. You can reassure them that it won't change their relationship with you or their father. Adding someone new into your lives won't change their feelings for their father or take his place in their lives. Instead, this will be an addition in their lives; another adult to do things with and to care for them. Reassure them that you wouldn't bring anyone into their life that doesn't treat them well.

This conversation will probably need to happen over time. The key is to be available to talk to them openly and to accept whatever they tell you without judgement. When you can stay calm and listen, you now have the availability to being to work through whatever issues come up.

It is going to be important to set some limits and guidelines with your children. You want them to be able to express themselves and know that you are listening and taking them into consideration, but you don't want them to think they can control your decisions. It is important to let them know that as the parent, you are ultimately in charge and will make the decision that you feel is best.

When you start dating, you could plan date nights with your children as well. This shows them that they are still important to you. You might go on a date Friday night but Saturday morning you do something special with your children. Put this on the calendar and stick to it. It can be something as simple as cooking a special breakfast that next morning. They look forward to those times and realize that your dating isn't taking away from their relationship with you.

Now that you are ready to date, where do you meet someone new?

Your time is already limited with work and taking care of children as a single mom. Who has time to look for a new partner? Consider joining one or two social groups where you can combine fun social time with meeting other singles. You might do this through a church group or meet up groups. This also gives you a chance to practice skills you haven't used for in a while, like flirting. You can also try online dating. It is a safe, time efficient way to meet new people. You can start with an email and a phone call from your own home. This way you have a better idea if this person is someone you want to meet before you hire a babysitter to go out.

When you first meet someone new you only need to share the basics about your situation. The first few dates are about getting to know each other. You do not have to share details about your children or your past relationship. That can come in time once you decide if this is someone you will spend more than a couple of dates with.

You and your date may need to be more flexible in the dating experience when children are involved. Phone calls in between dates can be a good way to stay in contact and further the relationship between dates. If the guy you are dating isn't understanding of your need to put your children first, he is not a good match. That being said, you do need to carve out time to date in order to build a relationship.

A question that comes up frequently is when to introduce your children to someone new. You want to be careful not to bring someone into their lives that might be another loss for them. My advice is wait until you have dated long enough to agree that this relationship has potential to be something permanent. I don't believe there is a specific amount of time but more of a decision based on where the relationship is with the person you are dating. This should be a decision you make together with the person you are dating.

When I was dating my now husband, we had been dating about 5 months before he met my children. At that point, we were both committed to the relationship and saw potential for a future together. We started off slow with him coming to dinner and then watching a movie together. We gave my children time to get to know him and adjust to him being a part of our lives. It is important not to rush this step or get discouraged if things do not go well at first. Slow and steady makes for an easier transition. Younger children generally accept someone new faster than pre-teens or teenagers. With older children it is important to be understanding and supportive of their feelings while setting limits to their behavior. Let them know you respect their feelings and they must respect your decisions when it comes to dating. It is ok to limit the contact an older child has with someone new. Don't force them to spend a lot of time together. Allow the relationship to grow slowly over time. A general rule with your children can be that they do not have to like the person you are dating but they must show respect.

How do you know who to date?

When you are deciding who to date you must consider your requirements in a partner as well as who will join you in parenting your children. They need to be a good match for you and your children. If they have children of their own, what is their relationship like? What kind of relationship do they have with their ex-wife? When I was dating my husband, I observed how he related to his children. I listened to stories about how their lives together when his children were younger. This played a role in my ultimately choosing to marry him. He was very respectful of his ex-wife and his children. He was calm and loving around them. I learned that this was someone I could co-parent with. After all, he was going to be in my home parenting with me for a long time. Don't overlook this step in deciding if someone will be a good partner for you. Make sure you talk about what his role will be in your children's lives. Do you have similar parenting styles? The divorce rate for second marriages, especially when you add children to the mix, is higher than for first marriages. It can be difficult enough for two people to blend their lives, but children add another layer to that mix. Making sure your values match goes a long way in avoiding difficulties later. In the beginning, you should retain the primary parenting responsibilities for your children. A solid relationship needs to be established before the other person becomes an authority figure. I always suggest being very cautious about leaving your children alone with someone new.

Don't rush into a new relationship. Consider dating a few people casually until you are ready to make a commitment. Practice your dating skills, compare personalities, and learn more about what you want in a partner.

Things to ask yourself before you start dating:

Have you made peace with the divorce and dealt with any feelings around the loss of your marriage? Or, do you have feelings, thoughts, and beliefs you still need to deal with?

If you are newly single, have you and your children adjusted to your new life together? Rushing into a new relationship too soon may not be right for you or your children. Give yourself some time to adjust to being a single mom, and give your children time to adjust to the new relationship with their parents.

Can you prioritize your children's needs and date at the same time? Do you have time and energy to commit to adding someone new to your life? Dating takes time and it means time away from your children, especially in the beginning when you are meeting new people. Can you fit that into your schedule and still give your children what they need?

Have you talked to your children about dating? Are you ready to deal with their feelings and reactions? Remember to take things slow and not introduce someone new into their lives until you have decided to become a couple and are relatively sure this is a relationship you plan to stay in.

Have you taken time to understand your relationship requirements and what you need and want from a new partner? Do you have an idea of what qualities in a partner make a good match for you and for your children? This is a good time to start doing some reading, listening to podcasts, or talking to a professional about co-parenting before you start doing it.

When you do decide it is time to date again, allow yourself to have fun and to enjoy the journey.

Dena Skoko

Dena has 25 years of management, leadership and program design and delivery in the personal development field along with her strong desire to make a profound and lasting difference in the world. Dena worked for a personal development company for 20 plus years facilitating and supporting hundreds of people in living life fully and designing lives that they love.

Dena now owns her own Coaching Business since 2016 and works with people both professionally and personally. She has supported many people in changing careers, manifesting the person of their dreams and in building their confidence while being powerful in their lives. She also facilitates Relationship workshops and works directly with couples providing conflict resolution, creating what's next in the relationship and creating the relationship so each person's needs are being met.

Dating after a Toxic Relationship
By Dena Skoko

Dating after toxic relationships

So how do we get ourselves in a toxic relationship?

It's likely one of the following occurred:

The relationship moved too quickly, and you didn't take the time to know the person before becoming intimately connected. When people get into relationships they often get swept up in the attraction. Then the temptation to get intimate comes and we jump into bed. Then the oxytocin gets released for the woman and the perception gets blurred by the chemical bond. It is best in my professional opinion to get to know who you are with before adding this element.

Many people worry about if they are going to be compatible in bed and yes I think this is important, however you can always work on that area down the road.

You stepped over the early warning signs:

It's good to note that people are on their best behavior in the beginning. So how do you find the signs of who someone is? I find that watching their interactions with service people is a great one. If they treat the people when you are out well that can be a good sign you're with a healthy person. Also, you can see how they are with their family and close friends another good sign. Usually people who will end up being toxic for you will have a few times where they slip. Be on your toes. Watch and listen closely. Ask questions. If you notice they are drinking a lot or working long hours, ask them directly "Do you think you might have a drinking problem or are you a workaholic?'.   Men tend to answer questions directly.

You missed noticing a main component:

Who are you when you're with this person? Do they bring out good and healthy parts of who you are, or do they bring out your dark side? I believe that a good match for us will bring out our best selves. We have so much attention on our excitement and glorifying the person in the beginning because we are in the new exciting part of the relationship, we don't look at this aspect. If you aren't happy, fulfilled and they aren't bringing out the best in you is it really a fit. Perhaps you missed this.

It's easy to blame yourself for bad relationships. It's true, you chose the relationship and it's possible you missed some early warning signs that could have saved you from the heartache and pain you suffered and may have you feeling down about yourself, dating and love. It's normal. Start by forgiving yourself. Be proud that you have taken a huge step by reading this book, which means you're ready to get serious about healing yourself and finding a healthy, loving relationship.

In order to do that, it's important to understand how you ended up in an unhealthy (Toxic) relationship in the first place and to begin the forgiveness process.

Let's start by getting a blank small notebook and make a list of everything you noticed in the beginning of your relationship that you now see as a red flag (i.e. something that bothered you, or wasn't in alignment with your values or way of life) – This is really important as we often overlook important issues early in relationships because we just want to enjoy new found love. Ask yourself – has this happened in past relationships as well? If so, you can begin to see your own patterns.

Next write out a list of what you liked about the relationship and what you didn't. Label the book with the person's name. It allows you to get it out of your head and in the book instead. I find this to be a great way to allow you to let go of brooding over the relationship. Toxic or not it still will linger on unless you put it in a place out of your head. Every time something shows up just take the book out and add to it. It's also good to realize we have all gotten involved at times in relationships that didn't serve our highest good.

Add a section to your book and call it the forgiveness section. List everything that you did in the relationship that you could now forgive yourself for. For example, "I forgive myself for getting in relationship with this person even though I knew they had a drinking problem" or "I forgive myself for letting this person put me down in front of others and for not standing up for myself". Make this list and add to it when you see other things you could forgive.

Next step is to take a good look at your relationship to yourself. Make a book for yourself and begin to write out your own lists of qualities you love about yourself, things you might want to change and ways to work on them. It is important to love yourself, so you are available to love another. When you look in the mirror are you someone you would want to be in relationship with. Being single is the perfect time to fall in love with yourself again, build the life you want to live (single or not) and create the space for the right person to join you, not fill in the void. Do great things for yourself and give yourself some pampering. Take some time to reflect and enjoy your alone time. Do some fun things. Take a trip or retreat. This is a time of reflection and completion. You will know when you are ready to move on. It's important to trust your gut and instinct. You are great and deserve self-love and self-care. When this process is complete you will know it. Some people say it takes ½ of the time you were in the relationship to complete the relationship fully and

I believe you can do part of that while dating. Getting out within a year of the end of your last relationship should be ample time. You don't want to get cold feet from staying out of the game too long.

Following getting your relationship to yourself in a good place. Next would be your relationship to dating and men. If you are not in a good place it will show and impact your effectiveness. It may be a culmination of this relationship and past relationships. So how do you get in a good place when you feel resigned or disenchanted? Stop and do some forgiveness. Whatever the situation was you should know that people ultimately are good inside. Your toxic partner inherited their behavior and did what they did because that's what they were taught. As the saying goes the apple doesn't fall far from the tree. So forgive them. Forgive their upbringing. And as I said earlier forgive yourself. This is an important step. The last thing you want is to repeat the cycle. Forgiveness is crucial. It is our access to being free. If we hold on to our resentment we suffer. Do whatever you need to do to get this phase resolved for you.

Now you're ready to date! You've forgiven yourself, you've forgiven your ex(s) – it's helpful to look at as many past relationships you can, even with your friends and family. It's time to clean out the cobwebs of the past and create your future.

Most people don't date well, often because they don't like the process. If you have that belief, change it! Dating can be fun and it's an important step in finding your perfect partner.

Why is dating important and necessary? Well it has two great purposes. First it allows you to get to know what you like and want. If you never went shopping for example you wouldn't know what was available. Secondly, it allows you to see "Are we compatible?". Does he have the attributes and enough similar likes that we can create a good relationship? The great thing about dating in the 21st century is we can do it online. This means you're not running from event to event trying to find potential single people. The downside of course is you need to meet many people to find a few that are a good fit for you as you don't have the initial in person oh wow, I like him.

The next step I recommend is get your Man list created. What are your preferences, non-negotiable, what's negotiable etc. What are you looking for? Its great to write this down and create what you are looking for. You can reference it later when you are dating a high potential person. You go and look at your list and see if the person is what you created. It's a check and balance system. I also find when you get clear it has you ready for the right person to come in.

After a toxic relationship getting back into the dating game with diligence is extremely important in my view. Perhaps the dating part is where you find who people are and see the signs that you either missed or stepped over. Maybe the dating process being slowed down a bit will be a way to take care of ourselves and to be able to select a great mate. In life we often rush into things and I have found slowing ourselves down makes us more effective in all areas of life not just pursuing a relationship.

Once you have done the work in this chapter you should have cleared out much of the negativity and baggage. Now it's time to jump in and start dating again.

Geoff Laughton

Geoff Laughton, an internationally in-demand Relationship Coach and Expert, known as Your Relationship Architect, is also the author of the internationally best-selling books, "Instant Insights on Building a Conflict-Proof Relationship" and "Built to Last: Designing & Maintaining a Loving, Lasting, and Passionate Relationship." For the last 21 years, he's been guiding couples & individuals in designing and building the conscious, Spirit-led relationships and life they truly desire. He is also the CEO and lead facilitator of The Evolving Man Men's Community.

Far too many people settle for what they believe is just the best they can hope to get. Geoff is devoted to guiding and mentoring people in how to have love relationships and lives that go beyond settling to instead create truly expansive, harmonious connections that heal and expedite those dreams that people have simply neglected and/or forgotten over time. A great amount of what Geoff teaches and guides people through has come from Geoff's own adventures in his marriage of 36 years.

To-date, Geoff has worked with thousands of private clients and couples; has led over 300 workshops around the country for singles and couples; and has spoken at numerous live and online events.

Dating After A Toxic Relationship – How Do I Search for Peace After Going Through Hell?

By Geoff Laughton

In today's world, dating and relationship, at best, can seem like navigating a mine field. When you've just escaped a truly toxic relationship, venturing back into dating can be some seriously scary territory to step into. However, if your heart's desire for a relationship is persistent and demanding this of you, there are a few pathways you can take to really optimize your likelihood of going through a repeat of what would probably be yet another toxic relationship in a series of them for you. Why do I say that? Because, we are creatures of patterns and habit, and until we get wiser to a few things about ourselves, we tend to attract the same kinds of people as lovers/partners…over and over again. Therein lies the first pathway to help you begin to start having non-toxic relationships.

Dating Yourself

The first thing you really need to do when coming off of a hellaciously toxic relationship is to follow the timeless advice of "Know Thyself." If you've endured a toxic relationship (or a few), it's because your relationship with yourself is toxic. The likelihood, particularly if you're a guy, is that you've been pretty conditioned to NOT know yourself inside. We are trained to define ourselves by our looks, by how well we can provide, how good we are in bed, how often we get laid, how hard we work at anything, how athletic we are, and – most toxically – how much we achieve out in the world. That is often what men tell me when I ask them, "Who are you?" Hell, that was my automatic go-to for the first 35-40 years of my life whenever someone would ask me to tell them about myself…name, badge, serial number, and job title. That is what SO many men I've met over the years use as a key part of their identity, yet you are SO much more than that.

Another trap that you can often inadvertently get yourself in is picking partners that you think will, in a way, fill in the holes or gaps in what you don't really know about your Self, or may even complete you in some way…a construct that the movie Jerry Maguire perpetuated that's essentially horse puckey. So, you will save yourself an enormous amount of unnecessary heartache and suffering by taking a period of time (I recommend at least a few months after you've gotten out of a really bad relationship) to only date yourself. What the hell does THAT mean, you're probably saying to yourself?

It means that you go on an intensive self-exploration to get clear answers to the following questions:

- ❖ Who am I REALLY?
- ❖ What are the 5 things I most appreciate and love about myself?
- ❖ What do I consistently try to deny about myself?
- ❖ What part did I play, and can be responsible for, in the failure of any past relationships?
- ❖ How have I re-enacted dynamics I grew up watching and feeling in my parent's relationship in my own relationships?
- ❖ What are my top 5 life values?
- ❖ What are my top 5 relationship values?
- ❖ What's my relationship to and with change?
- ❖ How much integrity do I operate in day-to-day?
- ❖ What are the three most important things to me in life?
- ❖ How do I expect a relationship to fulfill on those three most important things in life?

The first one is a bit of a trick question, in that the answer IS your lifetime's experiences and insights, so the answer is always evolving (or not). The rest, however, with some effort, honesty, and some reflections from those who know and love you most, can be achieved. When that happens, you will attain a level of self-awareness that leads to a greater clarity about what you actually want that's healthy in life and relationship.

When I've had to do this to better know myself, I've found it essential to have a few components in place: first and foremost, find a men's group that you resonate with. While you're the only one who knows what you know about yourself at this point, the support of some kind of community (besides friends, who can often be reluctant to reflect uncomfortable truths you really need to know back to you is crucial! Other conscious, awakening men can see things about you that are just blind spots to you and can offer a level of loving truth and support that we dudes just flat out need. Staying the Lone Ranger stunts your growth and development as a human. Two sources you can check out to find a men's community to start with are The Mankind Project (www.mkp.org) and The Evolving Man Men's Community (www.theevolvingman.com), both of whom have circles available to men around the world.

I'd also encourage you to go get a full, thorough check-up (especially getting your endocrinology system fully checked through blood work) to be sure that your body is operating at full strength, including your brain and hormones…especially if you're in middle age or older. This made an ENORMOUS difference for me in how I feel about myself. Taking great care of your body will put you on the path to self-love, particularly if you feel lacking in that at the moment (which enduring a toxic relationship dings up pretty badly, usually).

Lastly, get a professional guide/mentor who's walked enough of this kind of growth path to be able to show you options, guide you through the pitfalls you're likely to encounter, cheer you on when you want to say "Screw this," and tell you what you need to hear that you don't want to, so you can succeed. If you're working with a therapist already, a coach can be a great help in keeping you on track towards measurable results. If you're not in therapy, and don't feel that you're getting too bogged down in your mind, but just need direction, support, and accountability, then a life coach can be a great option. When I was going through a horrific mid-life crisis in my mid-30s (which many many guys do, by the way, whether they realize it or not), an incredible Coach I met helped get me through it so well that it totally inspired me to leave a corporate job I hated and become a Coach myself, which brought a love and passion for myself and my purpose to me that I'd lost any hope of having. You could start asking the friends you know and admire most if they know of a good Coach, they can refer you to.

I Think, Therefore I AM (NOT!)

The philosopher Descartes said that in the 17th Century. Most of us humans, when asked "Who are you?", will answer automatically with what we DO first. I could write an entire book or three on why it is that YOU are neither your mind nor your body. That is what your ego wants you to believe. Our ego wants us to identify AS our ego, and I'm a big proponent of who we actually are is our unique Spirit. You don't have to believe in a higher power to get (especially if someone you loved has ever died and you've been with their body after their Spirit had left the building, so to speak) that you have a Spirit. Some refer to that as their "Higher Self" or "Higher Knowing." It's the part of you that has intuition, can notice when you're screwing up and – in your head – go WTF?! We all come into this life with a Spirit inside that KNOWS the right things to be and do, along with a sense of purpose that's inherently available to know as we mature (and consciously look for it or allow it grow clearer as we grow).

It is essential that you get a bead on what your purpose is because that can be your most truthful inner GPS for your life and your relationship success. Too many people make having a relationship their life purpose, and it ain't! It can be a wonderful reflection and supplement to your purpose, but it can't BE your purpose. When you have a good sense of what it is, then you'll be more likely to attract partners that will be as inspired by it as you hopefully are and will be thrilled to support you in living it full-out. If you're attracted to someone who could care less about that…RUN!! How do you find out what it is, if you're not sure? Start with looking at what just consistently turns you on and/or pisses you off to the max, consistently. I had a coach once who told me that another great starting point for clarity on purpose is to go back and look at what your favorite things and play activities were when you were four or five. When I first heard that, I thought B.S.! However, once I thought about it more, I remembered that one of my favorite things when I was five was listening to the adults talk about life, problems, etc. So, 30 years later, I found myself (without planning on it at all) becoming a Coach, which I've loved with all my heart for the last 21 years. Going to www.thepassiontest.com can also help.

You won't learn who YOU are, or what your purpose is, solely in your head. I don't (and neither does anyone else I know) connect to my Spirit in my head. Our egos will be content, till death do us part from this Earth, to keep us living in our heads. One of the best books I ever read that helped me really get this concept was Michael A. Singer's book, "The Untethered Soul." You are hardwired to have emotions and feelings. While they are both part of our egoic structure, our emotions, which are of the heart and mind, are the closest relative truth that we can have in these bodies. So, all the conditioning that SO many men have had to regard their feelings and emotional needs/desires as something to be hidden so we look strong, is THE most toxic relationship we could maintain. You want to cultivate a strong, balanced intimacy with your heart, Spirit, body, and mind. The feelings are in there…our job is to allow them to come up, feel them, and then be released so you can stay present in present time. That skill alone will make an enormous difference in the quality of love partner you can bring in after you've been through hell with past partners. In that regard, I encourage people to get more familiar with their body through things like dance, yoga, or through watching an inspiring film and tracking what emotions it brings up. To better get you connected to the difference between your ego and YOU, find and maintain a meditation practice that works for you. It often isn't easy, at first, because the mind doesn't WANT to get quieter. But, I can tell you from my own experience, if you do it consistently, it WILL be a game changer for you, and help you connect with why you're here.

Eating Conflict Up for Breakfast

This is the final piece to get you into a strong position for relationship (and life) success. Many people abhor conflict, and will do anything to avoid it, including abandoning themselves in their relationships. Sound familiar at all? So, it will be a game changer, as well, when you develop a relationship to conflict that it allows it to grow you and your partner, rather than relating to it like it's akin to the anti-Christ. Conflict is NOT a problem…it's a fact of life. It's doing a piss-poor job of it that creates the problems. Most of us aren't taught how to do conflict with any kind of mastery. So, rather than indulging my tendency towards false modesty, I'd invite you to get ahold of my best-selling book, "Instant Insight on Building A Conflict-Proof Relationship." It's a short, very practical guidebook that teaches the basics of doing conflict well, with practical tips anyone can start practicing right now. Before you get into your next relationship, or if you're in one that's feeling bad to you because you're conflict avoidant, practice getting better at it with non-romantic relationships in your life.

Add all these together, and you will build a stronger, happier, healthier, powerful, and self-sufficient self, that will no longer tolerate or contribute to toxic relationships of any kind. Most of us who have repetitively found ourselves in crappy relationships have done so because we don't know ourselves very well, and – at an unconscious level at the very least – we don't LIKE ourselves and/or feel we're loveable. So, before getting re-engaged with a partner (or to get re-engaged in a new, healthier way with your current partner), start rebuilding the foundation of yourself that will guide you to the best and hold you up in times that feel like the worst…with or without a love partner. Enjoy getting reacquainted with your Self!

Laura Menze

After spending 13 years in the paint industry, with her last corporate position as a Global Marketing Communications Manager, Laura felt unfulfilled. She found coaching and her calling after taking just one class and decided to incorporate a business while working full time. Then, two months later, she was laid off. Rather than trying to find a new position at the height of the economic meltdown of 2008-2009, she decided to fully focus on building her business, and never looked back.

As a Professional Certified Coach, Laura coaches' clients in all areas of their lives and specializes in helping singles find, create, and keep an amazing love. She's all about helping create more love in the world. She's the Chief Love Officer at her company, Ready-Match, the host of The Radical Love Summit, a featured coach on the television series, Radical Dating – Breaking Through the Barriers to Find Lasting Love After 40, a Professional Coach Trainer for The Relationship Coaching Institute, Emily Makinzie's Love Guru on Denver's Mix 100.3 FM, and an Ordained Minister who's marries her clients who've found love. Originally from Chicago, she lives in Denver, CO near the mountains she's always loved.

Ready for Marriage Never Been Married and You're Finally Ready for the One! – For Women

By Laura Menze

As a woman who's never been married, missing milestones such as getting engaged, getting married, buying a house with someone, or having children, left me feeling left out, passed by, like I didn't belong, or knowing where or how I fit in life.

I struggled with feeling alone and unwanted. It seemed like everyone else around me was 'following protocol.' I began to question myself and wonder what was wrong with me.

I remember feeling lost in my mid-thirties. I had a good job, a dog and cat, and I actually purchased my first home.... all on my own, which gave me a great sense of pride, accomplishment and success in the career/success part of my life while feeling empty, discarded, and extremely unsuccessful in the personal/relationship part of my life.

I held corporate positions in companies that were dominated by men and felt the glass ceiling on the top of my head. I knew I wanted to be married, have kids with the right man (I knew I didn't want to have kids on my own), and start my own business when, one day, I realized that I was waiting for someone else before I could begin my life. It was a shocking revelation for me. Somewhere along the way, I picked up the belief that I needed to be married to really start my life. Once I realized I had this limiting belief, I knew I had to examine just about every other belief in my life. So, the journey in personal growth began. If my journey sounds similar to yours and you've never been married but want to be, here's where yours can begin too.

What Are Your Limiting Beliefs?

We all have a plethora of beliefs, most of which are hidden in our subconscious and handed down from our families, friends, and our culture. Working with a personal coach or attending personal growth classes are some of the faster ways to uncover those hidden limiting beliefs which, even though you may not be aware of them, they are holding you back so, let's start becoming aware!

While waiting for a partner to start living your life is a very common limiting belief, some other examples of limiting beliefs that may be holding you back in your love life may include:

- ❖ All of the good ones are taken.
- ❖ I'm not… (skinny, pretty, smart, young, rich) enough.
- ❖ There are not enough men and/or I don't know where to find men.

- ❖ I am not good enough.
- ❖ I don't deserve love and/or to be happy.
- ❖ I'm too… (old, unattractive, dysfunctional, unsuccessful, etc.).
- ❖ My ideal partner doesn't exist or is already taken.
- ❖ There is no such thing as a soul mate or true love.
- ❖ I must be realistic in my expectations and settle for less than what I want.
- ❖ I will be rejected if I ask for what I want, or say no.
- ❖ I will be abandoned if I care too much.
- ❖ I will hurt the one I love.
- ❖ I will be smothered or controlled.
- ❖ I will lose myself.
- ❖ I will be hurt if I trust.
- ❖ If you really know me, you won't like me or love me.

Of course, there are many more that will be personal to you however, once you've identified your limiting beliefs, it's time to shift them to a new belief. For example:

All of the good ones couldn't possibly be taken because I'm a good one!

I don't need a whole herd of men. I just need one, and they are everywhere!

Shifting a belief can seem challenging. That's why the help of a coach can make a huge difference however, you can shift these limiting beliefs on your own. Start with the affirmation that you want to believe but have difficulty believing. For instance:

Limiting Belief: I am not attractive enough

Affirmation: I am very attractive to men

Affirmations can work. It's a 'fake it until you make it' mentality however, try taking one more step and shifting the affirmation into the form of a question. For instance:

Question: What makes me so attractive to men?

By putting it into the form of a question, your brain goes searching for an answer/evidence, which helps you to begin to believe the new belief. So, when answering this question, you might come up with:

I have pretty eyes. I have a great smile. I've been complimented on my hair many times.

Once you have clarity about your beliefs, you can begin to make more conscious decisions for your life. Once you begin to make more conscious decisions about your life, you begin to become more confident, and confidence is the sexiest thing you can put on to attract a partner; a man!

Are You Clear About What You Want?

Like many of the women who are now my clients, I thought I was clear about what I was looking for. My list included, things like, kind, generous, a good communicator, etc. (Sound familiar?) What I've learned over the years is that I'm looking for someone who can partner with me in a relationship and, ultimately, I need to look for the things I want in a relationship rather than a partner; the things that will be offered by my partner. It's a subtle difference in perspective but a major difference for one's love life. This did two things:

1. I stopped shopping from a 'laundry list' for an ideal man, who probably didn't exist. When we do that, we tend to get a specific image in our heads that includes height, weight, build, ethnic background, etc. The truth is, Mr. Wonderful doesn't always come in the package you are envisioning but he is wonderful and perfect for you, if you remain open and unattached to a specific dream or fantasy man you may have conjured up in your head.
2. I started looking for a man who would be able to support the kind of relationship I really wanted to share with someone. The questions I started asking were much different.

For instance:

Instead of: Do you want children?

I started asking: Do you spend any time with children? What are you doing when you're with them? What do you wish you were doing? What do you like/dislike about children?

There is a vast difference in the questions that will shift your date from feeling interrogated to valued.

Taking the time to get clear about what you want in your ideal relationship and then going on dates with this information can be life changing; both for you and your dates.

Are you stepping outside of your box?

Another lesson I learned that I also teach my clients is that it's important to get outside of your box or comfort zone. Clearly, your comfort zone hasn't been working for you. So why not try something different?

For example, I'm personally not a big fan of country music but I went to a country bar that has a big dance floor and beginner lessons early in the evening. I learned some basic steps and then was asked to dance by several men, all of whom knew what they were doing on the dance floor, which made me feel like a woman. I was being spun and twirled around the dance floor by men who were confident, knew how to lead, and enjoyed making me happy in that moment. I may not have walked away with the love of my life, but the experience required me to be a bit vulnerable, open, and trusting, which was likely different from my normal approach and that created an entirely different experience.

Can you sort through potential mates quickly?

As I stated earlier, it's important to know what you want in your ideal relationship rather than your ideal partner. Do you know your Requirements, Needs, and Wants in a relationship? Do you know why it's important to differentiate your list into these categories?

Requirements, Needs, and Wants

Requirements – These are black and white things; things that the potential partner shares with you or doesn't; yes or no such as:

- ❖ We love dogs
- ❖ We are Jewish
- ❖ We don't do drugs

Needs – These are just as important as Requirements however, they aren't black or white; there's a lot of gray area with needs. A potential partner could share these needs with you but might be a bit more or a bit less than you such as:

- ❖ We like things neat and tidy (He could be a bit more or a bit less tidy than you but he is neat and tidy!)
- ❖ We are optimistic (He could be a bit more or a bit less optimistic than you but he's optimistic!

Wants – Wants are not required or needed but it would be nice if….

- ❖ He was handy around the house
- ❖ He was a good cook

So, why is it important to differentiate your list with these categories? The short answer is that you want to know right away if the potential relationship will work before you invest a lot of time and emotion into building a relationship. The longer answer is that, if he doesn't' meet your requirements, and you invest a lot of time and emotion into building a relationship, the relationship will eventually fail. Why, because the thing that you ignored is a huge value for you.

For example, let's say you are Jewish, and you meet someone who seems to meet all of your other Requirements, Needs, and Wants. He is amazing in every other way so, you ignore this Requirement. You get married. Perhaps you have a Jewish and Catholic combination ceremony, and everything seems wonderful. Now you are blessed with children and it's time to introduce them to your religion, which you never talked about with your husband. He doesn't want his kids raised as Jewish and he's not going to compromise. Boom! Major problem, and now you are many years into this relationship. Wouldn't you want to avoid this potential problem upfront if you could?

Screening and Testing

Now that you know your Requirements, Needs, and Wants, you need to learn the skillset of Screening and Testing.

Screening – Asking the right questions to determine if he meets your Requirements so that you can avoid a detour. Remember when I said I learned how to ask better questions? That's because I knew my Requirements and Needs.

Instead of: Do you want children?

I started asking: Do you spend any time with children? What are you doing when you're with them? What do you wish you were doing? What do you like/dislike about children?

Let's say I learn that he likes children because that's what he told me. Great! Now it's on to Testing!

Testing – Does his walk match his talk? It's probably not that he's consciously lying to you. Perhaps he does believe that he loves children so let's find out. Set up a date with him where there are children involved. Perhaps the two of you are babysitting, attend a family reunion, or visit a park with a playground when there are ton of children playing. How does he handle it? Is he laughing and playing with the kids or is he muttering something about 'bratty snot-nosed kids?'

By Screening and Testing your potential mates, you can avoid many detours, which is really important, especially if you are older or your biological clock is ticking.

Are you keeping your blinders off?

Let's face it. You don't want to make the mistake again of spending 3,6, or 12+ months with someone only to finally realize that you never should have been with that person in the first place. It was likely that you knew they weren't right for you from the beginning, but you chose to ignore many of the warning signs, including friends and family who didn't really like him. Why? Because you weren't clear about who you were, what you wanted in a relationship, what you will/won't tolerate, or you weren't confident enough to express all of these to your potential partners.

You can keep your blinders off very easily by downloading the Red Flags Dating Checklist. It helps you maintain objectivity and can be used on the first date, fifth date, 3 months into the relationship and more. As you discover more and more about your partner, it's important to check to see if you are staying objective or if he is starting to meet some of the warning signs.

Never Been Married

If you've never been married and feel like you are missing some of those milestones I mentioned earlier, it's time to get clear about who you are, what you want, how to sort through potential partners and keep your blinders off. It's time to learn some skills and knowledge around dating and relationships. The end result will either end in marriage with the love of your life, and/or living a life that you love so, you've got nothing to lose and everything to gain! Ready. Set. Date!

Jennifer Gaynor-Yaker

Dating and life coach Jennifer Gaynor-Yaker lives in Los Angeles with her soul mate husband and business partner Rich, who is the cofounder of her businesses Joytopia™, and Conscious Life Coaching. Jennifer has spent the last six years coaching clients all over the world, helping them to live their best lives.

As a veteran dater who spent over 20 years in the dating trenches and has been on over 200 first dates, Jennifer Gaynor-Yaker knows firsthand what it takes to go from dating disaster to relationship master. Since personally experiencing a complete transformation in her own love life, Jennifer has since helped hundreds of women and men all over the world transform their love lives and find their soul mates.

Jennifer is the creator of the online courses "Becoming a Soul Mate Magnet™ and "The Online Dating Success System™" She holds over 20 coaching-related certifications including (but not limited to) certifications in intentional dating and mating, relationship coaching, spiritual life coaching, EFT (a.k.a. "tapping"), hypnotherapy, Neuro-linguistic programming, and hypnotherapy. Jennifer is also a professional speaker and is frequently interviewed on the radio and online on the topics of soul mates, love, relationships, personal growth, and self-transformation.

Mastering the Art of Online Dating (so you can find "The One")

By Jennifer Gaynor-Yaker

I remember a time when I was so fed up with online dating, I pulled myself off the 3 sites I was on and said "enough!" I was so burnt out I never wanted to do online dating again!

I also remember a much happier time – just 6 months later - the first time I ever met my husband. We met online and had been chatting by phone for a couple of weeks. We both knew we had a great emotional and mental connection, which is why he told me prior to our meeting in person "If we are attracted to each other when we meet in person, this relationship has future". I will never forget the very primal but delicious feeling of attraction I felt when he walked into the restaurant where I was waiting for him. The enormous smile on his face told me he felt the same, and the rest of history. We have been happily together for seven years and married for five (at the time of this writing).

Prior to meeting my husband, I actually went on over 200 first dates. Majority of those were dates with people I met while online dating. Since my own personal success finally meeting the love of my life with online dating, I've helped scores of other singles find the loves of their lives. Majority of these clients of mine who have also found success in love also met their partners on line. Yet, many people still have many negative experiences with online dating. What gives?

In and of itself, online dating is neither good or evil, nor dark or light. Like many things, it's all about how you use it. The bottom line is, it is possible to find the love of your life through online means. Consider these statistics cited in an article in The Daily News:

OPICS

- **"One-third of married couples in U.S. meet online": study**

Marriages that start online may also last longer, according to the study.

WASHINGTON - More than one third of U.S. marriages begin with online dating, and those couples may be slightly happier than couples who meet through other means, a U.S. study out Monday found.

Online dating has ballooned into a billion-dollar industry and the Internet "may be altering the dynamics and outcome of marriage itself," said the study by U.S. researchers in the Proceedings of the National Academy of Sciences.

The research is based on a nationally representative survey of 19,131 people who married between 2005 and 2012.

"We found evidence for a dramatic shift since the advent of the Internet in how people are meeting their spouse," said the study, led by John Cacioppo of the University of Chicago's Department of Psychology. "1OPICS

If you want to be successful with online dating, there are a few guidelines that are helpful to follow.

First, let's discuss the pros and cons of online dating.

The following are excerpts from The Online Dating Success System™" coaching program I created to help singles just like you easily attract an ideal match.2

Online Dating: Pros and Cons

Pros:

- There are many possible matches for you to choose from
- It's easier to tell if someone is single
- It can be easier to get a date (since there are more options)
- You can set up filters for easier sorting

- Dating online, with its many options, can create an abundance mentality
- Approximately 1 out of 3 new marriages are happening from online meetings

Cons:

- Having too many choices can create overwhelm
- You may get unwanted attention (especially if your profile and picture have flaws in them)
- Answering messages can start to feel like a second job, burnout can easily happen
- You may spend time effort and still not be finding a match

That being said, how you present yourself and show up online can dramatically affect the types of results you will get with your online dating effort. There are a few main keys to increasing your chances of success. To make it easier to remember them, I created "The 10 Commandments of Online Dating Success"

The 10 Commandments of Online Dating Success:

1. Though shalt post photos that truly look like you
2. Though shalt be 100% truthful in your profile
3. Though shalt treat others with respect
4. Though shalt not tolerate any disrespect from others
5. Though shalt take measures to avoid dating burnout

6. Though shalt be authentic every step of the way
7. Though shalt not spend more than 3 weeks before meeting in person
8. Though shall not have settings for geography set up further than one is willing to travel frequently
9. Though shalt be honest, upfront, clear, and direct when not interested in someone
10. Though shalt meet up with people and stay curious and also have "eyes wide open"

7 Guidelines For Effective Online Dating Pictures

1. Have at least 5 photos up of yourself. The more, the merrier, as long as they are all quality photos. If you're not sure how many to post, I recommend posting between 5-9 photos of yourself.

2. The majority of your photos should be of you, and only you. Especially do not have photos of you and someone from the opposite sex (or same sex if that is your orientation). It does not matter if it is your sister, mother, brother, father, cousin, or opposite or same sex BFF – the people scanning your profile won't know that. People want to "Photoshop" themselves into your life, and they may find it harder to do that if there is already someone on your arm. Part of being ready for an intimate partner is making space in your life for them. You can start with your photos.

A word about animals: If you have a furry BFF that you have a great shot with, it's ok to post a pick with them, It will help others sort. (for example, if someone is a cat lover or hater)

3. Make sure your photos are clear and not fuzzy or too dim. It doesn't matter if it's the best shot in the world of you; if you're not clearly visible and it's not of good quality, it's a no go.

4. Your photos should not be older than 2 years old. I know this one's a toughie, because you may have photos from a few years ago when you were younger/more fit/and just gone Paleo/run a marathon etc. But you need someone who will love you as you are now, even if that means a few fine lines or extra pounds. I am 100% confident there is at least one person out who will love you as you are right now. If you made any changes to your appearance (such as cutting or dying your hair), your photos should be even more recent.

5. Have a close-up headshot as well as at least a ¾ body shot. This picture should be accurate and reflect how you really look now – not 10 years ago.

6. Your photos should not be glamour shots. That being said, they don't need to be you on your worst day either. They should look like a version of yourself you can replicate easily to go out on a date.

7. They should show your personality. It's a good idea to have to at least one picture of yourself smiling, unless you are the type of person who rarely smiles, but keep in mind numerous studies show that people who smile are perceived as more attractive then people who don't smile. Activity shots are great, but your first pic should be a very basic headshot or ¾ shot that focuses entirely on you and your personality.

That being said, a good profile is only about 5-10% of what it takes to be successful finding love. The other 90-95% is what's going on inside of you – your feelings, our thoughts, your beliefs about yourself, others, and relationships themselves – and how you communicate and how up in relationships. If you are continually having trouble finding the right mate, you may want to work with a good dating coach so you can truly be ready on all levels –mind body and soul – to show up as your best self and be successful in love.

Melette Evans: "Helping create happier lives one person at a time"

Melette is a fearless adventurer who wants to spend her life surrounded by creative, loving, passionate souls with whom she can work and play.

A humanist with a mind equally designed for science and the aesthetic, Melette has worked for over 30 years to enhance the lives of everyone she meets in many different ways. From caring for hospital Emergency Room and Surgical patients and their families in a compassionate manner, to creating exquisite home / work spaces that enhance the everyday living experience for her design company's clients; and protecting the privacy and security of companies and individuals with her technical computer skills, Melette's mission is to leave each individual she encounters with a positive experience, however small it may be.

A writer and visionary, she's the founder of Bevylife.com, a beautifully crafted website bringing together singles who desire the ability to make deeper and more meaningful connections within their communities. This resource that connects like-minded singles supports Melette's deep belief that everyone leads a happier life when they feel as though they matter and have a place to belong.

When she's not writing or working, Melette can be found in some far-flung country discovering new friendships, enjoying unique experiences and making new memories.

Marry Who You Want, Not Who You Need
By Melette Evans

Why get married? That is a question often asked especially by men and women aged 40 and up. These days when it is socially acceptable to have children without being married, to live together without this legal commitment, and to buy property and enter into other agreements without being Mr. & Mrs., Mr. & Mr., or Mrs. & Mrs., why do people bother to go through this process of legal coupling, if they don't need to? To explore that question you must look at the reasons why people get married in the first place.

For the purposes of this chapter and our discussion of marriage, we are focusing on single adults in a mature age group from about 40 years and up. Some of these singles may be considering marriage to have children, and some may have "been there and done that" and so are no longer wanting to be a parent at this point in their lives. While our text includes references to traditional marriages between a man and a woman, the same reasoning applies to a marriage between two men or two women.

When asked "What are you looking for in a relationship", many single men and some women searching for a partner will state that they just want a "committed relationship".

Often that statement is a clandestine way of saying they would like a steady partner and would consider living with them, but they are not interested in marrying them. When pressed further as to why they are not open to marriage, the answer that most frequently comes up is that there is no need to get married at this stage in life. Most adults in their 40's and up are not seeking a relationship to have children, and even if they are, it is no longer socially necessary to marry to become a respected parent. Most people in this age range have established some sort of work or career and do not have a requirement to be financially supported by a partner; they have their own money. And most men and women have at least one horror story to tell where they or their friend, relative or business associate did take the plunge and marry, and then wound up in a messy and costly divorce. Who would want to repeat that experience? Men and women who nowadays can lead independent lives in most everything they do, have all but erased the need for marriage. So why do it? Why get married when you don't need to?

When we talk about reasons for marrying, it may be easy to confuse the "need to get married" with "getting your needs met" from the right relationship. There is a big difference. The "need to get married" comes from a place of lack, a desperate sort of place. It comes from a place of over-dependency where one feels as though they cannot do what they want to do or be who they want to be, without the other person. There is a heavy, weighted aspect to that kind of marriage which has been referred to as "the old ball and chain". On quite the opposite end of the spectrum, there are certain needs or deal-breakers that everyone considers important in a relationship. Needs that if not met, the relationship would not be successful. Getting your needs met within the right relationship is very different than needing to get married. When your partner / relationship meets your needs, it is a very freeing feeling; you feel secure, happy, and respected. When your needs are not met, feelings of distrust, insecurity and depression can start to evolve, and over time will erode the relationship.

Wise parents often teach their children to "Know your wants from your needs", and this is can be good advice in many areas of life. Valuable lessons can be learned from carefully deciding where to spend hard-earned cash on things that you need instead of things that you want, so that money can be saved and invested for the future. But that same advice typically doesn't work in marriage. When considering marriage, consider "Marrying Who You Want, Not Who You Need".

So why are people who marry out of need rarely happy? There are a couple of reasons.

When you marry someone because you need to, it usually places an impossible burden on your partner. A secure and self-confident person does not need a partner to survive. A happy and secure person is complete on their own and able to take care of themselves without burdening a partner with the responsibility for their existence and happiness.

If a person marries out of need, as soon as that need is no longer there, the relationship often dissolves because the need that was the glue holding the relationship together, is no longer there.

So, what exactly is meant by marrying for want rather than need?

Years ago, I was introduced by my friend Karen to a recently married couple, Lindsey and James both in their early 40s. The minute I met them, I asked Karen what in the world they were doing together. Each talked about the interests and activities they enjoyed which were completely different from the interests and activities of the other. James hated the quiet, sedentary and solitary activities such as reading, needlepointing and puzzles that Jane loved. And Jane could not stand what she considered to be the excessive social nature of James's activities such as ski trips to the mountains with friends, dinner parties and foreign travel.

Each talked about long term goals they had, which directly conflicted with the goals of their partner. Both had achieved good positions in their careers, and both had previously been married and divorced. During their 30's Jane had wanted to become a mother as much as James wanted to be a father, but their previous failing relationships had eliminated that as an option. Single for a few years, Lindsey and James met through an on-line dating site and immediately felt a common connection of both wanting children. Once they met, all their conversations centered on how quickly they could get pregnant and how excited they would be once they had kids.

They married within 3 months of meeting and within 6 months were searching for an egg-donor since Jane's age prevented her from becoming pregnant without medical intervention. Two years and $130,000 of infertility treatments later, Jane gave birth to beautiful twin girls, and life was wonderful, for a short while.

Before the twin's first birthday, they were constantly arguing and each was complaining about the other, how they weren't performing the role each had expected of the other as husband and wife. It was not long before they were not even speaking with each other, and within 4 years they were divorced and having to navigate an acrimonious custody arrangement.

Lindsey and James married each other because they thought they needed to become parents, and without any real consideration as to what, beyond children, they needed from a relationship. Apart from children, neither had ever considered what they or their partner might need from the marriage to feel loved, supported and secure. James needed a wife to bear his children and Lindsey needed a husband to father hers. As soon as the children were born and that need was fulfilled, the relationship fell apart.

Had Lindsey and James married because they made a conscious choice that "this is the person I want to marry as opposed to need to marry, this is the person I want to be with, that I want to share my life with", they most likely would have never married each other. They would have remained open to finding a different partner with whom they could better relate and have the children they so desperately wanted.

Carole and Neal's story describes a marriage entered for a different need – a financial need and a need to not be alone. Carole was a business journalist in the early stages of her career, and though her professional future was bright, her current salary did not afford her the luxurious life-style that she considered important. She dreamed of being able to drive a Porsche, wear designer clothes and expensive jewelry and spend vacations in exclusive, high end resorts. Since she did not have the money to get those things for herself, she needed a husband to do that for her.

Neal was a very successful, young business owner of a technology company and was financially set. He had married a wonderful woman who unfortunately was diagnosed with Cancer soon after their marriage and had died a week after their third wedding anniversary. Though Neal was heartbroken at the loss of his wife, he shared with his friends that the very worst part was the fact that he was now alone and felt an enormous emotional emptiness. He could hardly stand it and was willing to be with anyone, do any activity, to have a distraction from the isolation he felt. He needed a relationship so he would not be lonely.

They met when Carole interviewed Neal for a story on his company that was to be published in the local business magazine. Neal saw Carole as someone he needed to fix his lonely existence. Carole saw Neal as the man she needed to provide for her material desires. I met Carole a few months after the interview and noticed the sparkling 5 carat engagement ring he had just given her. After congratulating her on her upcoming nuptials, I asked her to tell me about him, and was shocked at the way she described the man that was soon to become her husband. She started by saying that "He's not all that great looking and I've never really been attracted to him". When I then asked her if she loved him, she responded "He treats me well by giving me a lot of the things that I want", and she offered up the beautiful ring as an example of the material gifts he had showered upon her.

I did not get a happy vibe from our conversation that this marriage was going to go well. I got a similar sense of doom from a conversation that followed with Neal, when his description of her was limited to how he wouldn't be by himself any more once they married. Neither talked about love they had for each other, things that they had in common, or similar hopes, dreams and goals with each other. The relationship was all about getting married because each of them felt they needed to in order fix what was lacking in themselves, not wanting to get married because they had built a successful relationship together that naturally met each other's needs.

Carole and Neal made it to the altar, but not far beyond. A few months of living together as husband and wife began to wear thin on them both. Though Carole enjoyed the lifestyle that Neal could buy for her, she really didn't enjoy spending time with him, and was soon finding more and more reasons to be away from home, and away from Neal. Neal found himself back in the same situation that he had hoped to fix by marrying Carole. She was always gone doing who knows what, leaving him by himself and alone. Soon Carole found a new interest who could provide her an even bigger and better lifestyle than Neal had given her, and the divorce proceedings began.

When considering a relationship consider it from the perspective of what you really, really want in your life. Rather than look at outside needs as reasons to commit to someone, look within the heart for what it wants. The heart wants what it wants, and if you really ask yourself the right questions at the heart level, you will get the right answers. Do I want to be with this person, do I want to spend my time with them, do I want to live my life as an individual but shared with this other person? Marry for the reason of sheer wanting it. Marry who you want, not who you need.

Terance Tomsha

After a particularly painful breakup, Terrance Tomsha decided he had enough and started asking some different and uncomfortable questions. Questions like, who am I and why does this shit keep happening to me? Why is it so hard to find a relationship? In search of these answers, Terrance declared a year of living uncomfortably. Little did he know just how uncomfortable a year it was going to be.

Terrance sought out dating classes, took more therapy, and did a lot of reading. It was in a dating workshop that helped him realize that his life wasn't what he thought it was. It was then he discovered The Mankind Project, an organization with the mission of evolving the social and emotional core of manhood. After attending their New Warrior Training Adventure, his life was changed forever.

In the years since his MKP Training Adventure, Terrance has become somewhat of a personal growth junkie. He's taken more training with MKP and attends several workshops per year.

Terrance Tomsha is an award winning artist, an experiential designer, a car builder, and maker. His education includes a Bachelor in Mechanical Engineering and an MBA. When he's not creating, he's out attending live concerts, camping, snowboarding, and taking personal growth workshops

www.atomic-jellyfish-design.com

Never married, ready for marriage
By Terrance Tomsha

The real-life story of one man's (mine) journey from a salvage yard parts car to a fully refurbished '55 Chevy hot rod

The best metaphor to describe my life prior to 2010 is an automobile. I may have thought I've mastered how to rebuild, repair, hot-rod, and customize my ride, and yet I still managed to trash more than few vehicles in my life. The truth, however, is that I never felt I was in the driver's seat in the automobile that was my life. Always the passenger, never the driver. Oh sure, I had to grab the wheel once in a while to avoid some pants-shitting catastrophe. It always felt like someone else had the wheel and I was just along for the ride.

Who am I? Why am I here? Why does this shit keep happening to me? These were the questions that I woke up to in January 2010. The shit I'm referring to is another failed relationship. We didn't date that long; yet I still fell hard for her. In my head, I knew she was the "one". I saw the future; we were together, I could be a father to her infant son, and we would live happily ever after. Then she broke up with me. Turns out I was not emotionally capable of handling a breakup of that magnitude! My world fell apart. I was already working 10-12-hour days and 6-7 days a week for several weeks in a row. I had done a great job isolating myself from friends and family. I told myself that they don't want to hear about it or that they really didn't care. There were very few friends to talk to. Looking back, I wasn't even able to articulate what I was feeling, or to be more precise, not feeling. The vocabulary wasn't there. And yet, there was something inside me that told me not to give up and that I was destined for something more.

After several weeks of going through the motions and pretending that everything was just freakin' hunky dory, which also included several trips to my therapist. Reading books and bitching about it was only going to get me so far. It was time to take action and find answers to those questions. The year 2010 was declared "A Year of Living Uncomfortably"! Holy shitballs, I had no clue just how uncomfortable it was going to get.

Thinking that my relationship solution was a just a matter of learning a new technique, I enrolled in a dating class. About halfway through the class, the teacher made two lists. The first listed the things to "Do" in dating and then came the "Do Not Do". I nearly went apeshit after reading the "Don't" list. My way of being and dating was every single item on the "don't" list. The "Do" list might as well have been written in a foreign language because of how alien it was to me. After recovering from that kick to the head (and balls), it was clear that a different approach would be necessary. I was going to have to dig deeper for the answers.

These were the major actions that moved me forward and helped me grow the most.

Before you get started, here are some things I want you to know.

1. This is important for you to know. You are not broken. You are worthy.
2. Be curious
3. It will require you to get out of your comfort zone. Learn to be ok in the discomfort, it will pass and be replaced with resiliency.
4. Be sure to take care of yourself. Mind, body, and spirit.
5. Learn to be honest with yourself.
6. Start asking better questions.
7. Do this with purpose and intention. Do not do this half ass. (Go for the whole ass)
8. It's about learning to be a better man in the world. That's where she will find you.

Therapy

I believe that everyone should have a therapist. Here's a challenge, go through your contacts and count the number of professionals you have in your contact list. The numbers relating only to your health and well-being. How many? Is there a therapist on that list? Seriously, in today's world, that is a tremendous gift to give oneself. Find one that challenges you, not one that agrees with everything you say and then collects their fee. Pay attention to whether or not you are making progress. Set specific goals with your therapist so you can track your growth. One major thing I have noticed is that the more I take care of my mental and emotional well-being, my physical well-being improves as well. I have lost weight. Rarely do I get sick. Those little aches and pains that I pushed out of my mind or ignored have vanished, completely. Having one person who's objective and educated in issues relating to mental health and how to be human are paramount to my success in living the life I have today.

And yes, there are occasions that send me into a depression. It's taken time, patience, and a willingness to learn, I now know what my depression looks like, what sets it off, what helps sooth me, and what type of support to put in place. I have set up 3-digit text codes with several friends. When I need emotional support, I send out the text code. My friend then knows what I'm asking for and can be prepared. Also, if the person receiving the code is unable to support me, they have committed to responding with a "I'm unavailable" text. Life happens to others as well and an "I'm unavailable" response is perfectly ok. Discover what support looks like for you and then make good clear agreements. Today my bouts of depression are less frequent and shorter in duration.

The Mankind Project

I have held a man as he cried in my arms. There have been times when I have cried in the arms of a man, being supported. I wrote those previous sentences without shame, fear, or guilt. In fact, I wrote them with love, compassion, and pride. This is what healthy masculinity looks and feels like! A majority of what I learned about healthy masculinity has come from being involved with The Mankind Project. Their mission, "To evolve the social and emotional core of manhood". My evolution started by attending my first men's circle (called I-groups), which led me to attending their life changing New Warrior Training Adventure (aka the Weekend). As a result of this life changing experience, I have been called to serve as part of the staff on these Training Adventures. Being involved with the Mankind Project has been the greatest gift I have given myself.

Here are my top ten takeaways.

1. I am not alone in my struggles. This is first because it's the most important. Also, because it was the most profound thing I learned after attending my first Men's circle.
2. I got my balls back.
3. I learned that I could trust others. Soon after, I learned to trust myself

4. Healthy masculinity was taught, modeled, and practiced
5. To choose to live of service, integrity, and to hold myself and others accountable
6. That asking for help is a sign of strength
7. To accept and love all parts of myself, even those parts I judge as "wrong"
8. My creativity jumped a quantum level
9. Discovered a whole spectrum of emotions. It turns out that I have more than two.
10. I fell in love with all of me.

To find out more about The Mankind Project go to:

https://mankindproject.org/

To find out more about The New Warrior Training Adventure go to:

https://mankindproject.org/new-warrior-training-adventure/

To find out more Men's groups go to:

https://mankindproject.org/mens-groups/

COR Experience – Celebration of the Noble Man

It's one thing to attend a 3-day retreat for and supported by men. It's entirely different (wonderful, amazing, and humbling) thing to attend a retreat and be supported entirely by women. This was a powerful game changer for me and how I relate to women. It helped me let go of the bad habits, bullshit, and self-defeating behaviors that were preventing me from creating healthy relationships with women. In fact, after attending Celebration of the Noble Man all my female relationships changed, some got stronger and some had to end. While this retreat was more difficult for me, its still one of my favorites. The thing I find funny (or ironic) is that I could not have done this retreat if I hadn't done the New Warrior Training Adventure. That, and the fact that I found out about Celebration of the Noble Man while staffing an NWTA.

To find out more about The Celebration of the Noble Man go to:

https://www.corexperience.com/workshops-training-programs/noble-man/

Life Coaching

In my journey to be a better man I have used a variety of life coaches to help me grow in specific areas in my life. This is no different than hiring a batting coach to help you with your swing except that a life coach can help you step up to the plate in your own life! I realize that term gets tossed around and misused, so I'll just borrow this description.

"Part consultant, part motivational speaker, part therapist and part rent-a-friend, coaches work with managers, entrepreneurs, and just plain folks, helping them define and achieve their goals — career, personal, or most often, both."

- Newsweek

There's a lot of different ways the coaching can look. What I really liked and worked for me was a combination of one on one sessions and weekend retreats. The weekend retreats are my favorite because of the new connections I make (like-minded people who also like personal growth) and because having others sharing their stories and participating is heartwarming and healing. If you feel working with a coach is for you, do your homework and look for one. My recommendation is to make sure they have been trained and certified. Check their references and make sure it's a good fit for you. Here's a good starting point, The International Coach Federation, https://coachfederation.org/find-a-coach

Personal Growth and Development Workshops.

I'm using this section as a catch all for the random events I find as I move through life. These events can be a couple hours, one time only, or an introduction to a larger program. The important thing to remember is to get off the couch and out of the house. Here are some of the perks of attending personal growth events. There are almost always more women than men. More often than not, I am usually the only male there. If you're not careful, you just may learn something about yourself and grow. Better yet, you may find the partner you've been seeking!

I originally set out on this journey to win back the woman I thought was the "one," what I uncovered instead was something far more valuable and precious. I discovered my true self, who I am, without the labels, the judgments, and expectations. I now know what it means to be man, to model healthy masculinity. I stand for something larger than myself and will defend those who are unable. I have a confidence deeply anchored in my bones beyond anything I dared dream.

At this point, you may be wondering where the dating tips are, well, here it is! This is what is true for me. The more I know myself, what my needs and wants are, speak my truth confidently, maintain my boundaries, be vulnerable, be compassionate, and be funny, dating has become fun and rather effortless. When I'm out in the world just being me, the most amazing thing happens. Women just appear, everywhere, and then it's on me to take the lead. The last tip I want to impart on you is to be the leader you were meant to be. Women want a man to take the lead. What's important is to lead from the heart, not the head and knowing the difference between the two.

At the time of this writing my latest get out of the comfort zone project is (drum roll) theater! For the first time in my life I will be stepping onto the stage as an actor as part of the ensemble cast. In the dating realm, I have the honor of dating some of the most amazing women I have ever met. It's a whole new world of dating for me with lots of fun, honest and open communication, and yes, lots of amazing sex (with cuddling)! So I will leave with this challenge, go out and discover who you are meant to be. You're worth it! I know I am.

Sheryl Spangler

Sheryl Spangler is the founder of Heart & Soul Matchmaking and is passionate about helping singles find loving and lasting relationships. As a Certified Relationship Coach, Certified Matchmaker, and Online Dating Concierge, she believes that finding your ideal life partner one of life's greatest joys. Using skills she learned during years of corporate recruiting and coaching, Sheryl works closely with singles to help take the anxiety and guesswork out of the dating process.

Sheryl's unique approach is based on providing sound personalized guidance throughout the journey to help you avoid common relationship traps and derailments. With numerous successful outcomes to her credit, she helps you find your perfect match but more importantly makes certain you are "ready to be found." Whether that is through helping redefine your ideal mate, overcoming preconceptions or learning lessons from past relationships, Sheryl will help you lay the groundwork for finding your life partner.

Sheryl's warm and approachable style combined with business savvy will instill your trust and confidence. Her uncanny ability to determine fit and compatibility is remarkable. She found her ideal match online and if you use the tips outlined in the chapter, you can find yours too!

HOW TO BE A SUCCESSFUL ONLINE DATER
By Sheryl Spangler

Online Dating doesn't work!
Everybody lies in their profiles!
I don't want my friends to see me online!
People will think I'm desperate if I'm online!

Sound familiar? These comments are some of the biggest complaints I hear about online dating. But online dating DOES work. I know, because it worked for me and has worked for so many others.

Online dating can be a smart part of every single's dating strategy because online dating sites and apps offer "target-rich environments." Statistics tell us that approximately 20% of committed relationships and 17% of marriages began online. My guess is that these statistics are low—not everyone reports their experiences. For example, I met my husband online and never shared that with the service I used.

Whether you've tried online dating or haven't yet, please know there is a "method to the madness." This chapter gives you an online dating success roadmap. I encourage you to follow it closely.

Think about online dating sites as shopping malls. Would you go into stores that had messy window displays? Probably not. How about stores that didn't have anything you wanted or needed? Again, my guess is no.

Since you are the product in your "store front," make your "display" as appealing as possible to someone who might interest you. Your "store front" is your dating profile with pictures, and you're using it to draw attention to you!

Spend some time thinking about what you want in a relationship and who would be a good fit for you.

Some questions to consider –

- ❖ What is your relationship goal? Marriage? Long-Term Relationship? Casual Dating? Something else?
- ❖ What are your must-haves or requirements? Requirements are non-negotiable deal breakers. For example, if you want children, then you require meeting someone else who also wants kids. Or if you can't tolerate smoking, then you must exclude those who smoke.
- ❖ What distance are you willing to consider? Are you open to long distance dating or do you prefer someone in your local area? Define your local area in miles and think about what distance you'd be willing to drive for a date.

- ❖ What are some words or traits that describe your match?
- ❖ What age range are you willing to consider? For most, a 10-year range is agreeable. Try starting a few years younger than you are and going up from there. Statistics tell us that on average, women date candidates 5 years older and men date them 5 years younger. I blew the curve—my husband is 4 years younger, so don't feel confined by these averages. Choose the age range that works best for you.

Men, women think that most men want a much younger woman. If you do, then search for her, but be aware that many women with whom I speak specify a preference for younger men.

I have observed age misconceptions in both genders. Be open, look for interests in common, and meet the person regardless of chronological age.

Draft up a short, upbeat description that describes you and the person you're looking for. Length should be no more than 3 short paragraphs. When you're happy with your profile, show it to a couple of friends and ask for their opinions.

In online dating, photos are essential! Here are my recommended photo tips:

- ❖ Your pictures should be recent (within a year or two at the most). Be sure to caption the photos with date and location if applicable.
- ❖ Include more than one shot and no more than six. Lighting, perspective and environment affect how you look, so offer variety.
- ❖ Include a close-up of your face. Blurry images might give the impression you're not serious about the process or that you're hiding something.
- ❖ Include at least one full-body shot of you wearing something formal (as in a nice evening out) and/or something fun and candid.
- ❖ Include shots of you engaged in an activity you enjoy, such as hiking, biking, golfing, tennis, sightseeing.
- ❖ Who owns that arm slung over your shoulder? Don't draw attention away from you by including someone else, or parts of someone else. Don't use group pictures. You don't want to make people guess which one is you, or decide they prefer the look of one of your friends.
- ❖ Guys, if you're thinking of taking a shirtless selfie, think twice. Unless you're at the beach or pool, keep your shirt on!
- ❖ In general, people are attracted to others who exude well-being. Your photos can communicate vitality. Pick a "happy spot," under a tree, by the water or walking a path. A professional photographer can help put you in the best light and capture your "spark" in a creative

way. The overall look and feel you are shooting for is warm and approachable.

Ok, now you've got your profile set up. What's next?

Define and set up search criteria, save and run your search. Be as open as you can so that your search returns enough results. Aim for 200-300 prospects. You want enough prospects so that after sorting, you can find 2-3 to write each day.

Sort your search results by activity date. For paid sites, active members have the best chance to be paying members. On paid sites, only paid members can read and reply to correspondence.

Be the chooser. Ladies, online dating is an equal opportunity venue. If you like someone's profile and they're "online" or "active," then send a short icebreaker ending with a question. Try commenting on a photo and asking where it was taken. Or, if you read something in the profile that interests you, then mention it and ask a question about it. It's important to let your prospect know you read the profile and have an interest to know more.

Men, the ladies believe that you don't read profiles. Show them that you do by mentioning something in the profile that resonates and asking a question about it. You'll stand out for sure!

Reply to emails sent by people that interest you as soon as possible. By delaying, you risk missing the opportunity altogether.

If you're not interested, there is no obligation to respond. However, if you do respond, then make it short and general, and be clear that you do not wish to pursue a dialogue. Here's an example, "Thanks so much for your note. It doesn't appear that we're a fit so good luck in your search."

Match.com has a "no interest" link you can click, which is an easy way to say "no thanks."

Speaking of paid sites versus free sites—I recommend subscribing to one paid site and at least one free or specialty site. Ask your age-appropriate single friends and co-workers which sites they have used and like. If they haven't had success, don't let that deter you. Online dating success depends on many factors, including whether or not you believe that it will work for you.

Strive for progress, not perfection. You don't have to write perfect emails, and it isn't a good idea to expect others to do the same. There's no such thing as a perfect profile, initial message or message reply. There are a variety of ways to write profiles, draft messages and reply. Also, take spell-check into consideration when you are tempted to critique someone's typos. We've all been bitten by the spell-check/auto-correct bug. That said, do proofread your profile and messages to intercept errors.

Have realistic expectations of the process. Although your intent is to find and meet that special someone as soon as possible, it doesn't necessarily happen overnight. I recommend starting out with a 3-month commitment and then evaluating changes just before your subscription ends. Understand that all online dating sites have an auto-renew feature. Unless you cancel, your subscription will roll over and renew. When you do cancel, you'll get lower priced offers to stay as a subscriber, so by all means, don't allow it to renew automatically.

Many people won't respond to your emails, so set your expectation to that reality. Remember, on a paid site, only members can read and respond to correspondence. Others will pass because you do not fit their preferences. Preferences are subjective, so don't take it personally if someone passes you by.

Use Law of Attraction thinking. If you're going to date online successfully, you have to believe that it will work for you. If you don't, then it won't. Having a positive perspective and thinking optimistically are keys. Two Law of Attraction principles are "like attracts like" and "what is inside shows up on the outside."

Embrace the adventure of online dating. Be curious and enjoy getting to know people. Expand your physical preferences to see what is possible. Although attraction is important, a spark is something to build upon. Often, people become more attractive as you get to know them and appreciate their inner qualities, even if you were not visually bowled over at first.

You never know who may turn out to be a new friend or a business connection. When I was dating online, I came across the profile of man who didn't meet my requirements, but I was intrigued with what he did for a living. So I wrote, expressed that while he wasn't a match for me, I'd like to meet him and learn more about his business. We decided to have lunch, became friends, and ultimately, I wound up working for him. You never know what will come out of an online dating connection.

Remember the goal of online dating is to get offline. After exchanging 3-4 emails, someone should move the action forward. Ladies remember that online is an equal opportunity experience, so it's perfectly appropriate for you to suggest a phone call and offer your phone number if you're comfortable. Men, if you're suggesting the call, it's often a good idea to offer your number instead of asking for theirs.

Speaking of phone calls, Match offers a secure phone option if you wish to keep your phone number confidential. It's a premium service, so there is a fee. Google Voice is a great option, too, and it's free (https://www.google.com/voice).

A short phone call is a good next step that shouldn't be skipped. Sometimes the phone call can be painful, i.e. lots of pauses or nonstop talking by one person. Try to have a conversational question or two ready, in the event of a long pause, and by all means, gently interrupt the chatterbox. I remember being on an initial phone call with a nonstop talker. I eventually interrupted to ask if there was anything that he'd like to know about me. It may have been a shock to him, but at least I was able to participate in the conversation. If the conversation doesn't go well, don't feel obligated to meet. If asked to meet, then be honest and indicate that you're not a fit.

If the call goes well, then look at calendars and schedule a day/time to meet. I suggest coffee, a drink, or a walk for a first date. Try to limit it to an hour or less. The point of a first date is to see if you enjoy yourself and are open to a second date. If not, then thank them, wish them well and move on.

Don't fall into the trap of having the first date that never ends. If you meet and are enjoying the date, make a second date. I've heard stories of a first date drink that extended to dinner, and then extended to another activity. Often those types of first dates flame out quickly, especially if "romance" was involved.

When you meet someone you like, that's great. But it's important to continue meeting others. This may sound counter-intuitive, so let me explain. Too many singles meet someone they like and move too quickly into an exclusive relationship. There are great benefits to continuing to meet others, such as giving you the opportunity to compare and contrast to see who you really like and slowing down the process so you don't get serious too quickly with the wrong person. If you settle for the wrong person before you really know that person, Mr. or Ms. Right might be in your orbit and you wouldn't even know.

Persistent, consistent activity is a must if you want to be successful online. My advice is to try to spend 15-30 minutes a day online. Set aside a regular period of time to check your email, run your searches and send ice breaker notes, and read and respond to correspondence from those who interest you.

You will be a successful online dater if you decide that online dating will work for you, do it correctly and don't give up. The most important thing is to enjoy the ride. When you meet your match, it will have been worth it!

Joanna Shakti
The Soul Love Mentor of Ecstatic Intimacy

Joanna Shakti founded Ecstatic Intimacy, where she offers programs, events, and mentoring to men and women that empower them to put the hot and happy back into love.

Joanna says, "There are too many nice guys who "finish last," too many successful women who can't seem to find a great man, and way too many people who find themselves in the friend-zone!" As The Soul Love Mentor, Joanna inspires anyone who hungers for deeper love and intimate pleasure to find and create a relationship that is an expression of ecstatic authenticity, intimacy and ecstasy.

Joanna combines deep experience in masculine-feminine dynamics with her many certifications including Advanced Certified Tantra Educator, Accredited Journey Practitioner, Certified Partner Yoga Instructor, and Visionary Leadership Coach. Formally an Electrical Engineer with an MBA, Joanna now lives life to remind men and women of the power and potential of love – showing them how to reconnect with themselves and each other in profoundly loving, deeply intimate, and ultimately freeing relationships.

You may have seen her as the Intimacy Expert on America's Got Talent, or in her other appearances on Fox, VH1, and Comedy Central.

INTIMACY: THE GLUE THAT BINDS
By Joanna Shakti

Intimacy – the glue that binds a relationship – plays not just a critical role, but the most important role in lasting love. Maybe you equate intimacy with sex, maybe you equate it with deep conversations, maybe it means affection to you. It's all of that and more. If you want great sex and lovemaking, you need intimacy. If you want to be best friends and passionate lovers, you must be intimate. If you're seeking your soulmate, you must bring intimacy to your dating.

Let's start with the most common mistake singles make when it comes to love and intimacy. I hear this all the time from single men and women alike, "I can't learn about intimacy until I have a partner to practice with." WRONG!

If you want to attract a soul partner who will meet you heart-to-heart, body-to-body and soul-to-soul then you must learn how to be intimate before you meet. To be even more specific, if you want to be intimate with another, you must first be intimate with you. Now that we're talking about intimacy and you, I'll also point out the old, and very true, adage, "You can't love another until you love yourself." You see love and intimacy go together and they start with you.

Ecstatic intimacy and ecstatic love are ongoing and never ending. They are not destinations at which you arrive. You'll most easily understand and master this journey of intimate loving when you break it down into 3 phases. I call the first phase, the Activating Soul Love phase where you create an experience of "Ecstatic Authenticity" in you, which means it feels soooooo good to be you that you never again settle for less than your heart's desire. It means you give up ever selling yourself out or twisting yourself into a pretzel trying to make love work.

When you are Ecstatically Authentic, you are intimate with you. You clearly know your needs, wants, desires, turn-ons, turn-offs, boundaries and the like. You know yourself well and you're willing to show up and be seen as the man or woman you truly are. It means that you are willing to be seen in your beauty and your mess, your strengths and your weaknesses, your power and your vulnerability, your light and your shadow.

Although most definitions of intimacy include a description of a close personal, or even sexual, relationship with another, I take the definition much deeper. When you look at intimacy from a soul level, it means to know one another fully, without hiding, without pretending. Intimacy reveals the truth of body, heart, soul, mind and spirit.

Yes, real intimacy is risky. You must step outside of your comfort zone. It's revealing and exposing. It's vulnerable and that's exactly why it is the lifeblood of soulmate relationships. No other relationship has the richness, the depth, the power, and the transformative nature as that of this intimate union of souls.

So, the first step on the path of Soul Love is being intimate with you, so you can share your true self with another. A short hand way to look at this intimacy with you is:

In-2-Me-I-C

It means you look into you, know you, honor you.

When you share the genuine authentic you with another, then and only then, are you fully available to be love and be loved. When you open your real self – the good, the bad and the ugly – to another in relationship, then you can know you are loved for who your really are. Without this love and honor of self, you will never fully feel or trust another's love.

The hidden blessing in this self-intimacy and being Ecstatically Authentic is that you are most lovable and attractive to the ones who "fit" your heart and soul, when you're being genuinely you. You become magnetically attractive to the ones who are right for you. You attract them without effort, without trying. It happens naturally because you are being you – having fun, feeling confident. You're happy, with or without a date, and, by the way, when you're happy in your own life, your soulmate can walk in and make life all that much better!

Once you have that deep honor and love of you, once you have the ability to stand as who you truly are, you'll attract men or women who meet you, honor you, see you, and who are truly able to step into an entirely new level of intimate connection. At this point, you have crossed into the second phase of the Soul Love journey, the Loving Soul-to-Soul phase, where, by building on the intimacy you have with you, you can experience real intimacy with another.

Phase two doesn't require a relationship. It requires relating, which you do every time you meet someone new, share a conversation, or enjoy a date.

When you desire to love soul-to-soul you must create an experience of "Ecstatic Intimacy" where you let yourself be fully seen. You let the person before you look into your soul, to see beyond the veils, beyond the walls of protection, and into your essence. Ecstatic intimacy leaves no hidden secrets. There's no pretending to be someone you're not or pretending you like something you don't.

You actually learn that every time you sell yourself out, every time you tell the little white lie to keep the peace, or every time you put his or her needs before your own, you, little by little, destroy the relationship you find so precious. Over time, the love fades and the passion fizzles, not because there was anything wrong with either one of you or with the relationship, but it dies because you didn't trust yourself and each other to be real, to be vulnerable, to be intimate.

A short hand way to look at this intimacy shared with another is:

In-2-Me-U-C

You let her see into your soul. He lets you see into his soul.

Loving soul-to-soul means you live intimately day-in-and-day-out. You live intimacy in bed and out and you experience a depth of extraordinary love like you never imagined possible. You love each other more because of your "flaws," vulnerabilities, and imperfections. You love each other more because you're human – together.

With this kind of intimacy, men and women no longer have to be a certain way or play a certain role. They get to be who they truly are – owning their own desires. Let me be more specific. If you desire to be asked out, don't ask out. If you're excited and enlivened by planning a date, take the risk and plan a date. If you're excited and turned on by being courted, let yourself be courted. If you desire to ravish, do the ravishing. If you prefer to have your date pay for dinner, then don't volunteer to pay. That's inauthentic.

Now I caution you, if you pay because you want to prove your ability or because you don't like to receive or because you think equal is "right", or if you wait to be asked out because that's easier than being rejected, or you hold back your desires so you don't seem like a jerk, you are actually selling yourself out. You'll want to explore the Ecstatic Authenticity of phase 1 a little deeper.

Whether male or female, straight, bi, lesbian, gay, trans, or anywhere in between, you must allow the masculine and feminine energies of your sexual essences to dance and play together. It is these polarities of opposites that turns up the heat of passion and keeps the flames of love burning over the decades.

It's not time to buy into stereotypes, roles or expectations. It's time to be true to you, your desires, and your sexual essence so you can attract a mate who naturally fits, who makes you happy, without trying.

This means that if you have a feminine sexual essence you can truly open, soften and surrender. You can be supported and cherished. With this depth of intimacy, your feminine knows innately how to feel safe and receive the masculine.

At the same time, if you have a masculine sexual essence, you'll discover what it feels like to stand tall and strong in your mojo. You'll know when to wrap your arms around the one you love and when not to. You'll know when it's safe to open your heart into intimacy and when to soften into love.

Together, the masculine and feminine in intimacy create a deep bond of the heart that lives through and beyond the inevitable ups and downs of love. Ecstatic Intimacy turns conflict into communion and your relationship strengthens with every challenge you face.

Now as you're sharing that deep soulful intimacy, with your heart wide open, feeling cherished, valued, respected and admired, you move into the Living and Loving in Ecstatic Union phase. In this third phase you build on the marriage of authenticity and intimacy to create an experience of Ecstatic Ecstasy where you open up into the divine union of body, heart and soul and it feels so good – in bed and out.

Here you enter the realm of sacred sexuality, sacred sensuality, and even spiritual awakening. You will experience the realms of ecstasy and beyond because you know the recipe for true soul level love combined with physical level chemistry and passion that sets the two of you on fire!

The shorthand way to express this union with another is:

In-2-Me-U-R

You and I unite two as one.

As you connect and live in this realm of divine love, your relationship grows through treasuring, devotion, and reverence. You experience the union of human and divine in you and in another. You discover where heart and sex unite, and spirit leads.

You can enjoy the ecstasy of love. You simply have to step onto the path.

Ready-Set-Date invites you to step onto the path, to start getting intimate with you right now so that you are being the most genuine, and hence the most attractive, you. Honor you every moment of dating, every moment of relating. Tell the truth. Never settle. Don't be who you think you should be. Know that your one, the one who will make your soul sing and dance, is out there waiting for you to show up as YOU.

www.ingramcontent.com/pod-product-compliance
Lightning Source LLC
Chambersburg PA
CBHW060424010526
44118CB00017B/2350